Wholesome

FEED YOUR FAMILY WELL FOR LESS

Caitriona Redmond

MERCIER PRESS

IRISH PUBLISHER – IRISH STORY

Dedication

For Ma, Nana and Mam, who have taught and inspired me.

MERCIER PRESS

Cork

www.mercierpress.ie

© Caitríona Redmond, 2014

ISBN: 978 1 78117 202 5

10 9 8 7 6 5 4 3 2 1

A CIP record for this title is available from the British Library

Printed and bound in the EU.

Contents

Conversion Charts

I have a basic fan oven so all temperatures in the book are worked out with this in mind. Below is a handy conversion chart for you to use if you don't have a fan oven. Remember, however, that each oven is different. The more you bake and cook in the oven the more familiar you'll become with the hot spots and whether or not you need to shift cakes around if it's not fan assisted. Make sure you have a working oven light though, as often looking at what you are baking is possibly the best tool for gauging whether food is ready or not. I've also included some handy conversion charts for weights and measures on the next two pages.

Oven Temperatures

Celsius	Fan	Fahrenheit	Gas Mark
130	110	266	½
140	120	275	1
150	130	300	2
160/170	140/150	325	3
180	160	350	4
190	170	375	5
200	180	400	6
220	200	425	7
230	210	450	8
240	220	475	9

Volume

Metric	Imperial	Metric	Imperial
30ml	1fl oz	300ml	10fl oz
50ml	2fl oz	350ml	12fl oz
75ml	2½fl oz	400ml	14fl oz
100ml	3½fl oz	425ml	15fl oz
125ml	4fl oz	450ml	16fl oz
150ml	5fl oz	500ml	18fl oz
175ml	6fl oz	600ml	20fl oz
200ml	7fl oz	700ml	25fl oz
225ml	8fl oz	850ml	30fl oz
250ml	9fl oz	1 litre	35fl oz

Spoon Measures

1 tsp	5ml	3 tbsp	45ml
2 tsp	10ml	4 tbsp	60ml
1 tbsp	15ml	5 tbsp	75ml
2 tbsp	30ml		

Weights

Metric	Imperial	Metric	Imperial
15g	½oz	275g	10oz
25g	1oz	350g	12oz
40g	1½oz	400g	14oz
50g	2oz	425g	15oz
75g	3oz	450g	1lb
100g	4oz	550g	1¼lb
150g	5oz	675g	1½lb
175g	6oz	750g	1¾lb
200g	7oz	900g	2lb
225g	8oz	1½kg	3lb
250g	9oz		

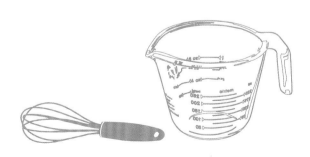

Acknowledgements

There are so many people I want to thank but I'm worried that someone may be offended at their omission, so rather than thanking loads of people by name here goes.

To the people who always believed in me, tried my food and weren't stinting in their honest feedback, thank you.

To my last employer, thank you for making me redundant. For a time I thought it was a huge disaster, but I know now that it set me on the right path.

To the people who (in good faith) counselled me to give up this blogging/writing lark. I hope you're glad I've proved you wrong.

To all the Irish Parenting Bloggers, who have been a huge support over the past year, I salute you. You are an amazing bunch and I'm so proud to be a member.

To the Irish Food Bloggers, who talk, eat and live food, thanks for making me so welcome and part of a great community.

To our family, in particular those who helped while I was shooting the book, thank you from the bottom of my heart – I couldn't have done this without you.

To the publishing team at Mercier Press, thanks for fulfilling one of my dreams.

To my readers, who comment, try my recipes, send me pictures, email me feedback, share the blog and are a huge support, don't let your budget get in the way of great food and thank you.

To Anne, Andy, Kathryn, Peter (the cake lover), Trish, Fran, Marie and Aunty Catherine, who each actuated an encouraging prod when it was required, you know what you've done.

Last, but not least, to John and Rebecca, Eóin and Fionn. I love you all so much.

Thank you.

Introduction

Gone are the days when I filled a supermarket trolley without a care for what it would cost when I got to the checkout.

It used to be that I selected whatever I wanted. I chose my shopping on a whim and tended to go with things that fitted around my lifestyle: convenience food, food that could be cooked in the oven or the microwave straight from frozen and eaten in my hand on the way to or from work. All of these things took a toll on my body and my purse, but I never really gave it much thought. I enjoyed food, but I didn't really care where it had come from to land on my plate, as long as it hit the spot and didn't involve too much effort.

Then, when the recession hit, I was made redundant, which forced me to take a fresh look at how the house was managed. Nowadays I run my kitchen like I ran the offices I used to work in.

There is very little I can control about our grocery budget, apart from what I buy with it. I'm restricted as to the amount I can spend on food every week. Thankfully, I have discovered that my choice as to what I spend it on isn't as limited as you might think. Good food doesn't have to be complicated or expensive. Fresh food cooked well and shared together becomes one of the most nourishing ways you can provide for your family and your soul.

This book should be treated as a manual for managing a kitchen on a budget. Take the recipes and adapt them to suit your own tastes. Use the menu planner to help you choose meals and fit them in around your lifestyle. You'll find the printable version of this and the shopping/stocktake template on my blog, wholesomeireland.com.

I wrote this book at the height of one of the best Irish summers to date. Yet the good weather didn't improve our financial situation. Over the course of the four months I spent writing and then photographing all the food you see here, our bank made a number of errors in their favour. I was left with fifty euro a week to feed our family of two adults, two children and a very hungry teen, until they sorted their issue out, which took over eleven weeks. Every single item you see photographed and written about was made within this weekly budget and we ate as a family meal. There is no such thing as a food stylist in my kitchen. Owing to the tight budget, I can't afford any wastage so no 'tricks of the trade' were used. I simply put the food on a board or a plate, photographed it and then we ate together.

If you have to live on a tight budget, are trying to save for a big occasion or simply would like to cut down on your food bill, there are key coping skills that you can learn that will help you to feed everybody a healthy, balanced diet.

The Stocktake

I would say that if we had a little bit more money to spend on food I'd be able to change the choices I make but, crucially, I wouldn't stop running the kitchen like a business. Managing the kitchen effectively cuts down on food waste and allows you to understand what you use on a regular basis and then plan for your spending accordingly.

Like every business, your kitchen has incoming and outgoing items. The grocery shopping is classed as an incoming item, and the food/products you use are outgoing.

It doesn't make sense to keep too much of an item you rarely use on your shelves, but it will cost you money if you don't keep your most commonly used ingredients in stock. I'm sure I'm not the only person who has run out of bread on an awkward day or time and had to pay more money to buy it from a convenience shop.

Stock rotation is also key. Most ingredients in the kitchen go off. Obviously 'best before' dates leave the canny cook with a little bit of wiggle room, but if you have 'consume before' dates on your fresh produce then you will have to throw them out if you don't use them before the advised date. Ingredients that end up in the bin are a waste of your money – you could have used it for something else I'm sure!

Changing your attitude to how you run the kitchen is the first step to it becoming a 'business' as opposed to just a room full of cupboards with food.

Set aside a few hours so that you can reorganise your cupboards. You can print off the handy stocktaking sheets from my website, wholesomeireland.com, to save you time (just click on the Free tab). Put on your old clothes and get into the back of your presses. Take everything out and detail what you have on the stocktaking sheets. Then get a big basin of hot soapy water and thoroughly clean the cupboards out.

Once you have done this, replace all the ingredients you have. Put the least-used ingredients to the back and the more commonly used ones to the front. At the very front should be (a) the most-used ingredients and also (b) those which have the closest use-by date. Don't forget that while spices do have a best before date, they are okay to use after the date but they do lose their potency.

If you find ingredients that you don't like or will never use, try swapping them with friends or family for ones that you will use. Failing that, your local food bank may accept these ingredients providing they are in date.

A stocktake is a huge undertaking and so I wouldn't recommend you do it more than once a month. It does, however, give you back control of what you use and when you use it. It makes it easier to plan your meals because you know exactly what you have and in what quantities. Simply believing that you know what is in your cupboards isn't the same. I'm very organised about what I buy and use, but I still manage to slip up and overbuy some items if I'm not keeping track of my stock levels.

So you've done your first stocktake. Well done, give yourself a pat on the back. Then take a break, because the next step is to come up with a realistic shopping list for the week ahead.

Calculating your Grocery Budget

How do you work out how much you have to spend on food a week?

Society nowadays has become tied up in paying debts, mortgage and committing to bills. Don't get me wrong, it's important to meet your financial commitments, but the first bill you should always pay is your groceries, then light and heat. Once you've allocated money for these three bills, you can divide up what's left between the rest of your responsibilities.

How much you should allocate for your food every week depends on your needs. For example, we rarely drink alcohol so never allow for that in our budget. If you have babies or toddlers in nappies then these will add to the cost of your weekly grocery bill.

In an ideal world, thirty euro per adult and twenty euro per child would be more than adequate to eat well for a week. We don't have that much, but that doesn't mean that we eat badly. If you feel that you spend a lot on your shopping and you're trying to cut down, use this rule of thumb to figure out what your ultimate budget should be for the week.

Once you've figured out your food budget, then factor in the non-food groceries. We still buy nappies and wipes, and then there are the cleaning materials, toiletries, bin tags … I could go on with this list. Give or take, I add a further twenty euro per week to our budget to cover non-food groceries.

My budget is ninety euro for the week for all my groceries, which leaves me with seventy euro a week to feed the family.

Compiling a Shopping List

Some people don't like the rigid form of a meal plan, preferring instead to eat what they like when they feel like it. However, meal planning is a good idea if you're busy, if you find you tend to have a lot of food waste, or if you like to shop infrequently, and it is absolutely essential if you are on a restricted budget. If you want to make a meal plan for the week you will find a simple template at the back of this book.

Whether you meal plan or not, a shopping list is an essential tool when you go shopping. It requires some discipline, but it will save you money.

I have a whiteboard in the kitchen with a wipeable marker on a piece of string. Every time I notice that I'm running short of an item, I write it on the board. The same goes for every family member. Mind you I sometimes find chocolate is scribbled on the board more than a few times!

Before I go shopping I get a pen and paper, then I write down the list in categories according to the type of items I need. The reason I do this is so that I am looking at the right part of my list when I'm in the various sections I'll be shopping in: dairy, bread, fresh fruit and vegetables, meat, frozen, tinned, baking … You get the idea. Once you've done a stocktake it becomes far easier to figure out what you need and plan what you will use in the week ahead.

With your shopping list in sections it'll make it far harder to be sucked in by flashy stickers and red-marked aisle ends which offer products that may not be as good value as you think.

Perishable products are replaced every week, for example milk. It's more than likely this will have a permanent spot on your shopping list. Other items like spices won't be used every day or maybe not even every week. Restocking spices, flour and less frequently used products is easy to do once you set aside five euro a week from your food shop. Every time I go shopping I stock up on at least three items, maybe sugar and flour one week and paprika and turmeric another.

I also buy nappies in bulk. I hate having to pay the full amount. I watch out for special offers and buy a few boxes at a time, depending on how good the offer is. This means doing a little bit of research before I go shopping to figure out where the best offers are and how much they're going to cost me.

A common piece of advice bandied about is to go from shop to shop to get the best value. This makes sense if you have time, energy and can afford the shoe leather/fuel to go from shop to shop. If not, like me, you'll stick to one local supermarket that offers the best value. Then it can be as much as four weeks between special offers so on the weeks that the 'nappy offer' isn't available, I stock up on other staples from my shopping list instead.

Store Cupboard Staples

Think of the store cupboard like the 'Superman' of the frugal household. It is my hero cabinet.

When on a tight budget I buy the same staples week in, week out. The reason for this is that I tend to have my shopping list honed to get the most out of my budget. This is where the spices, herbs and store cupboard tricks come in and change a standard plain meal into something memorable. It's also where I turn if I've run out of fresh ingredients or am trying to cut back on my spending in a particular week. You can be guaranteed I'll get at least one carbohydrate, one protein option and plenty of snacks from the press.

I wish I lived closer to a big urban area. I live near the north edge of County Dublin, quite a journey away from Dublin city centre, which is where the best spices can be bought for the best value in the Asian food stores. As it's expensive to make the trip just for spices, when I do travel in I make sure I have plenty of spare change and sturdy bags with me to carry my bounty home.

If you live near an Asian food store then you're in luck. A monthly or even quarterly trip and about ten euro should get you enough spices to keep you ticking over. You can also pick up bulk bags of rice, noodles and other essentials such as soy sauce, pickles and wrappers for making ricepaper rolls very cheaply. Of course, you will need help to get them to the house if you're buying that much. This is one of the reasons why my buggy has become a pure workhorse and some days I'll walk the toddler home so that I can use the buggy as a loading trolley!

I always have the following dried herbs and spices in my cupboard:

* Cardamom
* Chilli
* Cinnamon
* Coriander
* Cumin
* Garlic powder
* Ginger

* Mustard seeds
* Nigella (black onion seeds)
* Paprika
* Pepper
* Salt
* Thyme
* Turmeric

Dried carbohydrates always include:

* Bulgar wheat
* Butterbeans
* Cannellini beans
* Chickpeas

* Lentils
* Noodles (rice and wheat/egg)
* Oats (pinhead, milled and flour)
* Pasta (several varieties)

- ❀ Couscous
- ❀ Flour (wholemeal, plain, rice, gram)
- ❀ Kidney beans
- ❀ Rice (basmati and pudding as it doubles as risotto rice)
- ❀ Pearl barley
- ❀ Popping corn

Then there are the healthy treats that are cheaper than pre-packaged and boxed options for the family. Dried fruit in large bags bought in the supermarket is cheaper, gram for gram, than raisin snack boxes for a lunchbox. When fresh fruit is too expensive, I just bulk up our diet with the dried fruit instead.

The local health food store is ridiculously expensive, but when the dried fruit is nearing its sell-by date, they put it on a discount table near the door. I snap up the fruit then and use it in baking, then freeze the cakes, or rehydrate the dried fruit by soaking it in a little warm water or fruit juice and make a fruit sauce or compote, then bottle or freeze the sauce for another time.

When buying other staples like oils and sugar you need to keep an eagle eye on the prices. For example, my local big supermarket stocks caster sugar (a must for regular baking). The cheapest is their own-brand caster sugar. They have two different packages. The first is a plastic 500g package and the second is a 1kg package, which is made out of strong paper. The two packs of caster sugar cost exactly the same price, which means that it's cheaper, by weight, to buy 1kg than it is to buy 500g. When they are stacked on the shelf though, they are both the same height and breadth, with the package size marked on the side rather than the front. So unless you pick them both up, or can read the small print on the shelf label, you wouldn't be able to judge which was the better value.

I use a ginger and garlic paste in many of my recipes. A large jar in the local grocers costs me €1.49, but it is cheaper in the Asian food store. Where you see a teaspoon of the paste mentioned in my recipes, you can substitute 1 finely chopped clove of garlic and the equivalent size piece of grated ginger instead. Alternatively, peel and finely chop a full bulb of garlic and the same size piece of ginger, then add 3 tablespoons of sunflower oil and stir well. It will keep in a covered jar in the fridge for up to a fortnight.

Why Buy Fresh Instead of Processed Food?

Supermarkets and convenience foods don't make it easy on the budget shopper. I could feed my family on frozen pizza, chips and nuggets for the same cost as my weekly food budget. It's a difficult choice to make. Particularly when the amount of work involved in serving up a frozen pizza is far less than that of serving up a freshly cooked meal.

There are three key things you need in order to serve up fresh food on a regular basis:

* Time

* Skills

* Information

By educating yourself and getting used to having fresh food in your kitchen you'll find yourself less likely to pick up convenience food in the supermarket. And remember, the more processed your food is, the further away it is from its original nutritional value. It's also more likely to have come into contact with an increased amount of pesticides and herbicides, growth hormones and genetically modified elements.

There's an old saying that 'what goes in, must come out' and that can be applied to good and bad food. Everything you put in your body evokes a reaction. The more bad chemicals that have been involved in the production of your food, the more likely your body is going to be to react to these toxins. So, while convenience food may be quick to prepare and eat, more than likely every time you eat one of these meals your body will be feeling the effects for a long time.

One of the interesting things I discovered when I started digging down into the real costs of creating fresh meals at home was that, if you batch cook in bulk, it is cheaper to make your own food. Economies of scale mean that I can cook up enough baked beans to feed the family for two or even three meals for the same price as I could buy a tin off the shelf. I can roast a chicken, have a roast chicken dinner, make stock and use the remains of the meat for another two meals for the same price as four breaded chicken fillets.

Funnily enough, because you're living on a tight budget you have to think big when it comes to meals, rather than small. By buying in bulk when items are on special you will save yourself a fortune. That's why calculating your budget in advance is so important.

Savvy Shopping

Before you buy any fresh ingredients you need to have a realistic expectation of how long they will last in your kitchen, where best to store them to prolong their shelf life and whether you're going to use them before the produce is beyond eating.

There's no point in buying anything if you've no space to store it. Special offers will only benefit you if you're going to use all that you buy, otherwise you might as well burn your money before it reaches the till operator. Food not used is wasted food and this in turn is wasted money. You should be kicking yourself every time you throw out food that you can't use, particularly when the money to buy it is so hard earned.

For example, imagine you buy a bag of tomatoes for €1.50 and pass over an offer of 25 cent per tomato. If you only use two tomatoes from the bag and throw away the rest, that's a waste of the majority of a bag of tomatoes and a loss of €1 that you could have spent on something else.

On the other hand, I have a favourite brand of tea. It is extremely popular in Ireland and we go through an awful lot of it on a weekly basis. Tea is my only vice, as I rarely drink alcohol, don't smoke and try my best to keep baking to a minimum. I am determined not to spend too much money on it. The tea works out cheaper if you buy the smallest box possible, rather than the bulky large package. Again you'd only know that if you checked the price per gram weight on the shelf.

There are some ingredients that I know are going to be far cheaper to buy from the frozen section of the supermarket, no matter what the season. Frozen peas are a great example: they are so handy to have in the freezer all year around, they rarely fluctuate in price regardless of what time of the year it is and I can budget and plan my meals around peas as a staple ingredient every week. Likewise, sweetcorn tends to cost about the same price. Both peas and sweetcorn lose very little of their flavour or nutritional content in the freezing process, so in these cases I always buy frozen produce.

Berries are another frozen option to consider, as they will have been blast chilled to stop them sticking together in the freezer. The price by weight of frozen berries can often make it more economical to buy directly from the freezer section of the supermarket. However this does depend on the season and how well the local growers have succeeded with their crop. Do shop in the fresh food aisle first to see what kind of value you can get. The non-stick fruit can be mimicked by freezing the fruit in a single layer on a lined baking tray overnight and then decanting it into a freezer bag the following day. They should last for more than six months if well sealed and in the bottom of the freezer away from the element where they are less likely to get freezer burn.

I don't buy bread in the freezer aisle. I do, however, buy loaves of sliced bread on special and then freeze the whole loaf. Rather than taking out a full loaf of bread to defrost when I want fresh bread, I only take out what I need. If you tap a sliced pan lightly when it is frozen solid, each slice should easily come away from the next one. This means I always have a supply of fresh bread and never have any bread that is gone stale or mouldy.

Dairy products freeze extremely well too. I'm including milk, butter and cream on that list. If you notice them on special and have space in your freezer, then stock up when you can. Simply remove them the day before you want to use them and defrost in the fridge.

Until the beginning of this year I made do with a half-freezer over a fridge. It has three and a half drawers and I rotated my produce rigidly. Then, I managed to pick up a second-hand chest freezer on a trading website for a very small amount of money compared to the retail price. That week we ate very frugally, but the following week I had loads of space to store my freezer-friendly bargains. Keep an eye out where you can, as you can sometimes even pick up a chest freezer for free if you don't have one already.

Storing Your Food

You want to get the best out of the food that you have in storage and make sure it lasts as long as possible. Typically the jars, boxes and packets that you buy at the supermarket are not designed for longevity. In fact, I'd go as far as to say that they are designed to make sure that you run out of items pretty quickly.

Buying enough new storage is an expensive option – although if you can afford to stock up on plastic cereal boxes with pouring tops, kilner style jars and plastic lunch boxes with firm sealing lids, then by all means do so. It will stand you in good stead for the next number of years as you manage your store cupboards and food consumption.

There are other options to solid storage that are cheaper to get your hands on:

- ❊ **Bag clips.** These are sold in packets of twenty in an assortment of sizes. They are great for keeping packets clean and sealed, are extremely cheap and are easy to pick up.

- ❊ **Takeaway boxes.** While it might not be very often that you get a takeaway, when you do hold onto the plastic boxes that come with sauced meals. Give them a good scrub in soapy water before drying. They are perfect for holding two portions of dinner in the freezer or for prepared fruit and vegetables.

- ❊ **Resealable butter and ice cream boxes.** As above, give them a wash in soapy water. Invest in a black permanent marker to write up the contents of the boxes as they typically aren't see-through so it makes it harder to figure out what you have packaged away without opening them!

- ❊ **Milk cartons/plastic jugs.** These are great for holding onto dried goods in bags, once you cut the tops off and clean the insides out well.

- ❊ **Used jam jars and resealable bottles.** I put the word around that I like to take these. Every now and again a family member or neighbour drops me in a few and I pay them with a filled jar in return. Jars with lids hold sauces, jams, rice, pasta, spices, etc. There is no point in paying for them if you can get jars for free. Less than two euro will pick up over 20 jar tops for jam/preserve making that includes wax paper, pre-cut plastic toppers and elastic bands.

- ❊ **Biscuit or sweet tins that you get gifted at Christmas.** These are a good way of holding a number of jars at once and are stackable. If you don't get a gift of these tins, ask around to see if people are throwing any out! They're also great for holding jigsaws, Lego blocks and other small toys in the living area.

If all else fails, a couple of plastic sandwich bags and a permanent marker will do the job just as well. A maximum cost of €2 should keep you going with storage containers for a month or so.

Healthy Portions

I confess that I struggle with portion size and I'm sure I'm not the only person who does. As the world turned a bit and society evolved from the 1950s, at some point the average size of a plate became bigger. We started to eat off gigantic dinner plates, larger than an old record (remember those?). The thing is, these big dinner plates are fine, providing you don't fill them with food. Somewhere between our Irish Catholic guilt for starving children in Africa, and the land of plenty that the Celtic Tiger brought us, we started filling these plates with food – in fact, covering every spare inch with food.

Dinner plates are not meant to be filled with food. It is not healthy to eat that much and you certainly will be eating far too many calories in one meal, unless your dinner plate is filled with celery!

If you cover a large dinner plate with food, this food is going to cost you money, whether you eat it or not. If you eat too much food, you'll put on weight and be unhealthy – there is an ultimate cost. If you don't eat everything on a plate, then it's going to end up in the waste chain and again it has cost you money.

Reduce your portion size in a very easy manner by eating off 'tea plates' for main meals and 'side plates' for snacks and lunches. It is a visual reminder that you shouldn't pile your plate with food and yet you should finish what you serve up. Investing in some cheap tea plates will save you money in the long run.

Reduce the amount of meat protein you eat as a family. We require far less than we think to sustain ourselves in a healthy manner. In fact the average adult needs not a full breast of chicken but a half breast of chicken in a main meal.

Opt for more vegetables or fruit and reduce the amount of carbohydrates. I think when you're on a budget you are more likely to try to fill your belly because you don't want to feel that you're suffering on a frugal diet. So I tend to top up with carbohydrates like rice and eat too much of them.

If you're thirsty and you're not paying attention to your body signals, you may be more inclined to eat rather than to drink. Try to drink at least one glass of water with every meal and two drinks in between. If you don't drink enough you may get confused between hunger pangs and thirst.

I'm not suggesting for one second that you should starve yourself or scrimp on essential foods to save money. What I am saying is that if you don't eat to excess then you will be able to manage your food budget better, particularly on the weeks when money is harder to come by. You're not placing yourself in a situation where you expect oodles of food.

Discount Food

Food that is near its use-by/sell-by date is often sold by supermarkets and grocers at a reduced price. Recent times have seen the advent of the 'yellow sticker' which covers a barcode on an item, and a second reduced-price sticker. Theoretically you should find more yellow sticker items in a supermarket towards the end of the day, but that doesn't always happen because you won't be the only canny shopper checking out the usual spots in the supermarket.

There are some groceries that lend themselves more to buying from these reduced-price sections, so here are some tips and tricks to make the most of discount foods/yellow stickers:

- When you see eggs on discount in a big supermarket, buy them up. Larger stores have rules that eggs can't be sold beyond a week before their 'best before date'. In a supermarket eggs are kept in a temperature-controlled environment but not chilled. If you chill the eggs when you get home, they should last at least a further ten days. Just remember to remove them from the fridge an hour before using them in baking to allow them to return to room temperature.

- Meat is one to watch out for. Sometimes you will pick up a bargain and it will be grand if you cook on the same day or freeze immediately. However, not every supermarket has the same temperature control conditions so if you are in doubt at all do not buy meat on its use-by date.

- Battered tins, bashed cereal boxes and out of season products go on discount all the time with plenty of wiggle room on their best before/sell-by date. Nobody wants to buy Christmas pudding in July right? Wrong! Now is the time to stock up, leave space in your cupboard or freezer for these bargains and take the pressure off yourself for later on in the year.

Meat Consumption and Alternative Protein Sources

Are you a vegetarian? If so that's good news from a budget point of view, as meat is a considerable expense for any family. Do you have a 'Meat-free Monday' or 'Fresh Fish Friday'? These will also bring down the cost of your shopping budget.

As a rule it is a good idea to have a protein source with at least two of your daily meals. However, this doesn't have to be meat. Beans, pulses, dairy products and eggs are all a great source of protein and are far cheaper than buying fresh meat or fish.

You'll often see chefs and cooks on the TV telling you about 'cheap cuts' of meat. In my experience, when you're on a budget there is no such thing as a cheap cut. Cuts of meat like pork knuckle are indeed less expensive, but the reason for their cost is the amount of meat that is on the actual bone and the time it takes to break it down.

Minced meat is quite cheap to buy – extremely cheap if you buy it in the supermarkets. I buy my mince in the local butcher's, simply because I can see him make it in front of me. Minced meat bought in supermarkets may not be made in the same way and even though it looks the same in the pre-packaged tray, that's because it's been manufactured to give that appearance. In fact, supermarket-bought minced meat may contain a form of mechanically recovered meat, so I prefer to see it prepared in front of me. 500g of minced meat is enough to feed us for two full meals so I buy the larger amount and then break it down into smaller-sized bags when I get home and freeze the meat per meal.

It is more economical to buy a large piece of meat and then break it down to get a couple of meals from the one cut. A medium chicken will result in at least two meals from the meat, and a further meal from chicken stock. A small piece of beef on the bone will also give you a number of meals, and likewise you'll get a great nutritious stock from the bone after you've picked the meat from it.

When it comes to buying any food, the less packaging the better. Many butchers and supermarkets sell their meat on pre-packaged trays, which often includes a sauce or seasoning. As a rule I don't buy meat that has been pre-seasoned. I have small children, and exposing them to excessive amounts of salt at an early age is not a good idea. Too much salt/sodium can contribute to health problems. It's far better to wait and season your food at home or at the table, where you can control your consumption levels.

Irish legislation means that any manufacturer can take foreign meat, use sauces and dressings on it and then claim it was produced in Ireland on the label. The easiest way to check the origin and condition of your meat is to ask your butcher. It's far harder to hide the condition of the meat if you buy it without a sauce or a sealed package.

Beans are an extremely cheap alternative to buying a cut of meat for dinner. I'm not talking about a tin of baked beans, far from it. A bag of dried beans will last you for weeks. All you need to do is remember to soak the beans the night before you intend to use them. A portion of dried beans costs about a quarter of the price of a fresh whole egg, and a fresh whole egg costs about a quarter of the price of a piece of fresh meat. When you put it that way it's hard not to consider eating alternatives to meat when you are on a budget. Eating an egg a day is an excellent way to maintain a healthy level of protein in your diet.

Fish is also a great option when you're considering varying your protein intake to get costs down. While the likes of cod is pretty expensive in your local fishmongers, a whole fish is far less costly. People don't seem to like looking at a whole fish with the head still on. Ask your fishmonger for cheaper whole fish which you can cook on the bone to retain flavour, or for a bag of trimmings which can be made into a nutritious fish pie, rather than a fillet of cod or haddock.

Dried pulses do need to be prepared in advance, but get them ready in bulk rather than soaking and cooking every day or second day. Once cooked, they will keep in a sealed jar in the fridge for up to five days. Soak your pulses (chickpeas or dried beans) overnight in a covered bowl or pot. You will need about four times the volume of water to pulses. So for every 50g of dried goods, pour over 200ml of water. The following morning drain off any remaining water. Rinse the soaked pulses and cover again with 200ml of water and a pinch of salt per (original) 50g weight in a large pot. Bring to the boil and simmer for 1 hour. If you have bread soda in the house, half a teaspoon added to the boiling pot at the start will help your beans become more tender when cooked. Once the pulses have simmered for an hour, drain off the water and leave to cool before moving to the fridge. The cooked weight of the pulses will be four times the weight you started with. So if you see a recipe for 200g of cooked chickpeas in this book, you will only need 50g dried weight.

Essential Kitchen Equipment

It's always a surprise to people when I mention how small my kitchen is. I work in a tiny galley kitchen, storage is at a premium and so I don't have or work with masses of equipment. There are a few kitchen items that you can get by with. Every single recipe in this book has been made using a combination of the following equipment:

* Large, heavy-bottomed saucepan with steamer basket on top and firm lid
* Small saucepan
* Non-stick frying pan
* Two 35cm x 25cm baking trays
* Two 25cm diameter ovenproof baking dishes. I use ceramic, but cast iron is just as good
* Large wooden spoon
* Hand whisk
* Heat resistant spatula
* Two 18cm diameter sandwich tins
* 12 hole cupcake tin/muffin tray

- 1kg (2lb) loaf tin
- Sharp paring knife
- Vegetable peeler
- Large chopping knife
- Chopping board
- Large grater
- 22cm diameter cast-iron bundt tin (a large circular tin with a raised hole in the middle for ring-shaped cakes)

When it comes to electrical equipment you can get by with a sturdy electric hand-held mixer. I use a stand mixer, but that's simply to save on having to stand and hold a bowl. I also use a cheap stick blender, which is brilliant for pulsing soups and pastes. You can pick up both for under €20 in the supermarket.

I don't have a flashy oven. Mine is a bargain discount fan oven with two shelves inside. It also doubles as my grill so I can't use both at once! My hob is a bog standard four-ring hob. No bells and whistles, nothing expensive and so it's the same as you'll find in kitchens up and down the country.

My countertop is taken up with the draining board from my sink, the hob and then the kettle sits to one side. My chopping board fits very snugly between the hob and the sink. That's my workspace. I keep a box beside the chopping board so that I can peel/chop/prepare my food and discard any waste straight away for sorting into the compost bin when I'm finished. It reduces mess and makes it easier to clean up at the end of meal preparation.

Try to get your most-used tools and ingredients at easy locations in the kitchen. The harder it is to access them the less you're going to use them.

Extra kitchen equipment always helps and it's good to have more saucepan options, a griddle pan, more chopping boards and baking tins/trays. Do remember though that the more equipment, the more washing up, and you need space for it too!

The Emotional Toll of Living on a Tight Budget

'Ah sure it's easy, isn't it?'

'Well for you, at home with the kids, you can cook all day long if you want to.'

These are just a couple of the comments that I receive on a regular basis. Honestly

though, I find it very hard, and if I have any advice it is that you shouldn't underestimate the toll of living on a tight budget.

There are days when I find this way of life draining, exhausting and incredibly stressful. The last thing I want to do is to have to trek between supermarkets to get good deals or to stand at the stove for hours on end. I want to provide the best possible food for my family within the budget we have.

The day I was made redundant wasn't unexpected. What I didn't realise was how awful it was to be made redundant, how the word can make you feel. Redundant: beyond usefulness. Unemployed: without a job.

There are plenty of organisations that can help with claiming your entitlements, getting food if you can't afford to put any on the table and finding out where you stand legally when you lose your income. But there wasn't anybody there to show me how to run the house, how to cook on a budget, or how it didn't make nutritional sense to buy frozen pizza for two days a week, even if it did only cost €5 for the two meals that we ate pizza for. I'm now using the skills I already had to make the household work for us. It just took me some time to recognise that if I could organise a filing cabinet at work, I could organise a food press at home. If I could spend an hour shopping around on the phone to get the best quote for work, or looking for an insurance quote, then I could do the same trying to figure out how to save money in the house.

When so much of my life was out of my control, cooking and nourishing my family was something that I could control. It gives me great strength to be able to take ownership of and responsibility for the food we eat and where it comes from.

Bountiful Breakfasts

It's easy to get stuck in a rut of just toast or cereal in the morning, especially when they are convenient to make. I think that if you set a small amount of time aside you can start your day in a very special way. I'm not talking about slaving for hours to make the ultimate breakfast. After all, when you're trying to get kids out the door to school or get out to catch the train to work you really don't want to be stuck in the kitchen. Here are some easy breakfast recipes that can be eaten on the go, batch cooked in advance or are quick to whip up.

You can also refer to the Eggs, Spuds and Pulses section to find more multi-functional dishes that work at any time of the day.

Low-Sugar Blueberry Muffins

Blueberries are a super fruit to cook and bake with because they keep so well in the freezer and have a balanced amount of water in them, which means you're not going to end up with a sticky mess. A good alternative to blueberries are raspberries. If you'd like to use strawberries, make sure you chop them up into small pieces (about the same size as a blueberry). You can also replace the blueberries with two bananas, sliced or chopped into similar small pieces.

makes 12 muffins

260g plain flour • 50g caster sugar • 1 teaspoon baking powder
pinch of salt • 150ml milk • 50g natural yoghurt
75ml sunflower oil • 1 medium egg • 150g blueberries

Method

❋ Preheat your fan oven to 170°C. Line a cupcake tin/muffin tray with paper cases.

❋ Put the dry ingredients into a large mixing bowl and stir to mix them around.

❋ Combine the wet ingredients (milk, yoghurt, oil, egg) in a big jug and mix them together with a fork until they are combined. Pour slowly into the dry ingredients and stir until you have a thick batter.

❋ Add in the berries and stir one more time to make sure they are coated in the batter.

❋ Spoon into the muffin cases, taking care not to fill them more than three-quarters full.

❋ Bake in the oven for 35 minutes or until golden on top.

❋ Once cooled, these muffins will keep in a sealed container for up to three days.

Breakfast Bars

Let's face it, there are days when we don't have the time to take a long leisurely breakfast and I have been known to leave the house without any form of sustenance whatsoever, except, of course, my obligatory cup of tea. It can also be hard to persuade kids to eat what is good for them in the mornings and every now and again you can feel like you really don't want to do battle at breakfast time.

These breakfast bars contain all the same ingredients that you will find in a bag of muesli with the addition of a little butter to make them hold together in the oven. I make at least one batch a week and know that the kids are getting vital wholegrains, vitamins and iron, even if they do end up grabbing a bar as they run out the door for the bus.

The ingredient list is in 'American' cup measures simply because it's not so much a technical list but more an indication and you can add/subtract ingredients according to your family preferences. One cup is equivalent to about the 250ml point in a measuring jug.

makes 20 breakfast bars

1 cup rolled oats • ½ cup sunflower seeds • ½ cup hulled pumpkin seeds
½ cup raisins • ½ cup dried apricots • ½ cup dates, chopped
½ cup flaked almonds • ½ cup melted butter • 1 cup runny honey

Method

❋ Preheat your fan oven to 190°C. Grease a baking tray and dust it with flour.

❋ Combine all the dry ingredients in a large mixing bowl. Mix loosely with a wooden spoon. Pour in the wet ingredients (melted butter and honey) and stir until all the dry mixture is coated.

❋ Press firmly into the baking tray. Bake until golden brown and crispy at the edges. It should take approximately 25 minutes.

❋ Remove from the oven and leave to cool for 10 minutes before scoring the shape of the bars out on the mixture while it is still hot. This makes it easier to break when it is cold and rock solid.

❋ Wrap each bar individually in greaseproof paper and they will keep in a sealed container for up to a week in a cool, dry place.

Sugar-Free Energy Bars

I can't afford to be sucked into the breakfast bar section in the shops. As well as being ridiculously expensive, they are full of processed sugars. There are some sugars in these bars, but they are natural fruit and honey sugars so the bars are sweet without having the bad stuff in them. These are a very different kind of bar to the previous recipe as they are not baked or cereal based.

The more plump dried fruit is, the more expensive it becomes to buy. Bags of 'ready to eat' fruit have been semi-dried or pre-plumped to ensure that they are moist and not too dry. The most dried and wizened fruit will benefit from soaking anyway so don't worry too much if you have some pieces that feel like leather! Swap out the dried fruit according to your tastes.

makes 10 energy bars

5 dried prunes, chopped • 5 dried apricots, chopped • 30g raisins • 30g sultanas
50g high quality cocoa powder • 100ml hot water • 50g sunflower seeds
10g sesame seeds • 5 tablespoons runny honey

Method

❊ Take a large bowl, put all the dried fruit in it.

❊ Take a mug and measure out the cocoa powder. Using a little of the hot water, make the cocoa powder into a smooth paste, then add the rest of the water.

❊ Pour the cocoa water over the dried fruit. Cover the bowl and leave to stand for at least an hour, but overnight is best.

❊ Line a baking tray with cling film.

❊ Toast the sunflower and sesame seeds in a dry pan or alternatively measure out 60g of the crunchy seed mix (see page 205). Pour the seeds into the plumped up fruit, add the honey and using a wooden spoon (or a stand mixer if you have one), beat until you have a paste. The fruit will break down a bit.

❊ Smooth the paste into the baking tray. Cover with cling film and chill for 2 hours before slicing. The bars keep best in the fridge for up to 2 weeks.

Porridge

When I was little, my dad used to put the porridge oats to soak in the pot overnight and then cook it up in the morning. We always made our porridge with water, adding milk and anything else after it was cooked. Porridge is a super food for breakfast, low GI and very filling.

I prefer to make my porridge the night before, but nowadays oats are so finely milled you don't need to pre-soak if you don't want to. The beauty of making it in advance is that you can then reheat your porridge in the morning if you like it warm OR you can eat it cold.

Yes. Cold porridge. Probably not nice on its own, but absolutely stunning topped with fresh fruit and flaked nuts or coconut, then swirled with honey. Or even with a little fresh orange juice on top. It doesn't have to be the stodge of old that we remember from our childhood.

Mind you I still hanker after piping hot porridge with a drizzle of cream and a sprinkling of sugar and cinnamon.

per serving

40g porridge oats or about 100ml volume in a measuring jug

Method

❋ To make perfect porridge you'll need twice the volume of water as porridge oats. To speed up the cooking process you can use boiling water. Combine the water and the porridge oats in a saucepan on a medium heat, keep on stirring until the porridge bubbles, then turn the pot off, cover and remove from the heat. It will be fine overnight until you're ready to eat in the morning as you've only made it with water, not a dairy product. It's also fine to eat straight away if you want to, so you can make it in the morning if you have time.

Berry Smoothie

I keep a stash of frozen berries that I collected over the summer months in the freezer. I clean them with a vinegar/water solution (10ml vinegar per 300ml water) and then separate them into sandwich bags, each containing enough for smoothies for the family. When I'm browsing the over-ripe section of the fruit and vegetable section of the supermarket, I buy up brown bananas. Once home, I peel and chop them roughly, then add them to the bags of berries.

serves 4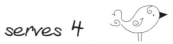

100g fresh or frozen berries – whatever is available
2 fresh or frozen ripe (or overripe) bananas, peeled and roughly chopped
700ml orange juice
60g/1 handful of porridge oats (optional)

Method

✻ To serve up the smoothies, take out the frozen fruit an hour before serving (or the night before), then blitz, using a stick blender, with the orange juice. For extra nutrients you could also throw in a handful of raw porridge oats. This makes a fruit and slow-releasing carbohydrate 'thickie', which will set you up for the day ahead.

Buttermilk Pancakes with Blueberries and Banana

Buttermilk is a magic ingredient in our house. Along with the baking soda, it provides all the rising and binding agent necessary in these pancakes, which then means you don't need eggs. This recipe is ideal for those with an egg allergy as the whole family can eat it together. I'm not a fan of preparing individual meals for various family members, far better for you all to cook and eat together!

serves 4

2 ripe bananas • 150g plain flour • ½ teaspoon baking soda • pinch of salt
75ml buttermilk • sunflower oil for frying • blueberries
lemon juice and golden syrup or honey to serve

Method

❀ In a large bowl, mash the bananas, then add the flour, baking soda, salt and buttermilk, and beat well. The mixture will be slightly on the lumpy side from the bananas, but don't worry, this is normal.

❀ Set the batter to one side to rest for 10 minutes. While it's resting, preheat a large frying pan with a teaspoon of sunflower oil on a medium heat. You don't want a high heat for pancakes.

❀ Use a tablespoon-full of the batter for each pancake. Cook a maximum of three pancakes at a time in the pan to make sure they cook evenly. You will need to top up the sunflower oil every now and again.

❀ Serve with lemon juice, syrup and some blueberries on the side.

Granola

I love muesli but I can't justify buying it in the supermarket when I can make it for half the price at home. The kids love this home-made granola and we eat it on top of pots of yoghurt, with a glug of milk or with fresh fruit cut into it. Traditional granola is made with some oil or butter. I skip that, which makes it suitable for fat-free diets and people with a dairy/lactose intolerance.

12 portions granola

200g rolled oats • 50g sunflower seeds • 50g hulled pumpkin seeds
50g crystallised ginger • 3 tablespoons runny honey • 50g dates, chopped
50g raisins • 50g sultanas

Method

❀ Preheat a fan oven to 170°C. Line a baking tray with non-stick greaseproof paper.

❀ In a large bowl, combine the oats, seeds, ginger and runny honey. Tumble onto the baking paper and use a fork to make sure it is spread evenly.

❀ Bake in the oven for 20 minutes. Toss the mixture around about three times during cooking.

❀ Remove from the oven, allow to cool and then add in the dried fruit. Toss together and keep dry in a sealed jar.

Pancake Pops

What child (or adult) doesn't like food on a stick? I've used cocktail sticks for these pancake pops, but if you're cooking them up for small children get your hands on some proper lollipop sticks.

Make the batter the night before. That way you're good to go in the morning and it's not all that difficult anyway!

makes 6 pancake pops

250g plain flour • 1 medium egg
100ml milk • 50g butter, melted

Method

❉ Whisk together the flour, egg and milk. Don't worry too much about lumps as they will settle overnight. Cover the pancake mixture and forget about it overnight.

❉ Before cooking whisk again, then whisk in the melted butter. This will stop the pancakes from sticking and you won't need to use oil.

❉ Heat a non-stick frying pan on a medium heat. Use a teaspoon to measure out the lollipops. When the batter begins to show bubbles on top, press the stick into the batter before turning the pancake using a spatula and cooking on the other side.

❉ Serve with a fruit jam or compote.

Baked French Toast Chips

My kids love French toast. It's called 'pain perdu' in French, which literally translated means 'lost bread'. It's traditionally made with stale bread and is a great way of softening hard crusts. When I have stale bread, I like to cut the crusts off and use the centre to make fine breadcrumbs so it leaves me with some crusts that I use for this recipe.

I'm a big fan of not standing in front of the hob if you don't have to. Baked French toast chips are quick and easy to make in the oven and because you bake them you won't need any oil in the cooking process, so it's healthier too!

serves 5

3 medium eggs • 30ml milk

stale bread crusts or 'chips', cut to equal size (about 6 crusts/chips per portion)

tomato relish (see page 206) (optional)

Method

❀ Preheat a fan oven to 180°C and line a baking tray with non-stick greaseproof paper.

❀ Take a large shallow bowl and mix the eggs, milk and some salt and pepper together with a fork until they are combined. Dip the crusts into the batter and roll around until they are fully coated. Lift up and hold over the bowl to allow any extra batter to drip off before placing each crust onto the baking tray. Make sure that there is a little bit of space around each crust.

❀ Bake in the oven for 15–20 minutes. They should become golden brown.

❀ Serve with a side of tomato relish and a salad if eating for brunch or lunch.

Banana Melba Toast

There's no better way to start your morning than with a banana. They are full of potassium and natural sugars. They are also low GI, which means they help to maintain your energy levels until lunchtime. Bananas can be hard to digest later on in the day, so I prefer to eat them first thing. The melba toast adds great texture to the dish too.

serves 5

40g butter • ½ teaspoon ground cinnamon • ¼ teaspoon ground ginger
4 ripe bananas • Squeeze of lemon juice • 10 slices sliced-pan bread

Method

❊ Take a medium saucepan and melt the butter at a low heat, then sprinkle in the ground spices.

❊ Peel and slice the bananas into chunks, taking care to discard any stringy bits. Add to the melted butter, then squeeze over the lemon juice. Stir until coated with the butter and leave on a low heat.

❊ Toast the bread on both sides until a pale golden colour (not too brown). The best way to do this is in a toaster but a grill is fine too.

❊ Taking a sharp knife, remove the crusts on all four sides (you could then use these for French toast chips – see page 43). Place the trimmed toast flat on a chopping board. Put the palm of your hand on top and carefully move a serrated knife through the middle so that you have two very thin slices of bread from one slice.

❊ Toast again until dark brown and serve with the cooked banana.

Bountiful Breakfasts

Fruit Samosa

While these fruit parcels would make for a lovely dessert, we like to pair them up with some low-fat fromage frais for breakfast instead. Because they are baked, not fried, they are low in fat and, by using my reliable stock of frozen fruit and no sugar, they help keep down our sugar intake. The best sort of fruit to use is frozen berries, but peeled and chopped banana, apples, pears, mango, pineapple or plums work just as well.

serves 5

270g pack of ready-made filo pastry • 100g frozen fruit (no need to defrost)
30g butter, melted • fromage frais to serve

Method

❈ Preheat a fan oven to 190°C and line two baking trays with non-stick grease-proof paper.

❈ Using a sharp knife, divide each sheet of filo pastry into three strips, lengthways. Put a tablespoon of the fruit on one end of a single long piece and fold the end over diagonally to make a triangle. Keep folding the pastry over, turning at a 90° angle with every fold. Once you reach the end of the piece, tuck the loose end to the bottom and place on the baking tray. Repeat with the remaining pastry. You should end up with about ten samosas, allowing for a certain amount of torn pastry along the way.

❈ Brush the samosas with melted butter and bake in the oven for 15 minutes until golden brown and slightly bubbly.

❈ Allow to cool a little before serving with a dollop of fromage frais – they are just as nice cold as they are warm though!

'Guggy' Egg

We enjoy this breakfast dish any time of the day or night. In our family it has magical qualities. I don't know what it is, but both myself and my husband have fond memories of receiving an egg in a cup, or a 'guggy' egg, as a treat and as comfort food when we weren't well. It is easy on the stomach and a good way to get protein into picky eaters.

serves 5

5 medium eggs • 30g butter • black pepper
hot buttered toast to serve

Method

❋ Place the eggs into a pot of cold water and bring the water to the boil. You don't want these eggs to overcook, so the minute the water starts to boil set your stopwatch for 3 minutes.

❋ Line up five mugs and put a knob of butter in each of them, followed by a crack of black pepper.

❋ When the stopwatch reaches 3 minutes, remove the pot from the stove and put it straight in the sink. Don't bother pouring out the hot water. Turn on the cold tap and let the water run directly into the saucepan. Run the tap for 90 seconds.

❋ Carefully remove the wide end of the egg over a mug and, using a teaspoon, scoop out all the contents into the mug. Mash with a fork and stir well.

❋ Serve with buttered toast.

Home-made Pop-Tarts

If I had the money and I let the kids choose their food in the supermarket, I've no doubt that a version of a Pop-Tart would land in the trolley. I first tasted them in the Middle East, a few years before they landed in Irish stores, and to this day I feel they are far too sweet, not to mention the long list of ingredients on the side of the packet. There is a little preparation involved in making home-made Pop-Tarts, but if you invest in 'toaster pockets' which are extremely cheap to pick up in your local value store, you can freeze the partially cooked tarts in the pockets. Then all you do is pick out a frozen pocket and pop it in the toaster for a quick, wholesome and nutritious option!

I tend to use my store of frozen berries for filling, but you can also use chopped banana, mango, pear, apple, pineapple or plums. To increase the iron and fibre you can chop in some dried apricots as well.

makes approximately 10

300g shortcrust pastry (see page 242, Jam Tarts – double the recipe)
plain flour for dusting • 100g frozen berries • 30ml milk in a cup

Method

❀ Preheat a fan oven to 160°C and line two baking trays with non-stick grease-proof paper.

❀ On a flat surface, dusted with flour, roll out the shortcrust pastry to a square or rectangular shape about ½cm thick. Using a sharp knife, divide the pastry into ten rectangles.

❀ Using the knife, score a line down the middle of each rectangle so that if you are looking at the rectangles, it may look like a book – with pages on either side.

❀ Divide the fruit evenly between each of the ten rectangles, filling only one side of the scoring line and leaving about a 1cm gap at the edges. Brush the edges with a little milk and then fold the empty half over the full half, before pressing the ends shut with your fingers. Now you have a fruit and pastry parcel.

❀ Bake in the oven for 20 minutes. The pastry will look pale and white but not translucent. Remove the parcels from the oven and allow them to cool before placing each one into a toaster pocket and freezing.

❀ To serve, remove individual pockets from the oven and toast on high.

Soda Farls

I always thought that there was a secret to making soda farls. You rarely see them in the shops and when I do buy them I find they are hard as building blocks.

There is no secret! The reason why you can't buy decent soda farls in the shops is because they are nicest when freshly made with a runny egg on top and maybe a couple of bits of crispy bacon too.

makes 4 big soda farls

300g plain flour • 165ml buttermilk • 1 teaspoon baking soda
pinch of salt • flour for dusting

Method

❀ Place a non-stick frying pan on the hob on a medium heat.

❀ Put the flour, buttermilk, baking soda and salt in a large mixing bowl and mix together until you have a loose dough. I normally do the mixing with the back of a knife or a fork. The key is not to overwork the dough.

❀ Pull the dough together into a ball with your hands and place on a well-dusted chopping board. Dust more flour over the top. Pat the ball down so that you get a flat, round shape, about 2cm in height. Cut the dough into quarters.

❀ At this stage the frying pan should be at a constant medium heat. Put the four pieces onto the pan and allow them to cook until golden brown on the bottom. At this stage flip the farls and cook again on the other side. You will notice that the sides may appear a little raw. Once the two big sides are cooked, turn all the farls on their side and rest against one another, turning until every edge is cooked.

❀ Serve immediately.

Mam's Brown Bread

This is one of the very first recipes that my mam ever learned. She went to school in a convent and the nuns were insistent that the girls they taught knew how to bake bread and cook hearty meals, amongst other skills. Over the years she has tweaked and added some extra ingredients, but overall this is the one that she returns to again and again.

The original recipe that she passed on to me had a combination of imperial (ounces) and metric measurements. I've converted them all to metric and it still works just as well.

makes 1 loaf

225g coarse wholemeal flour • 30g wheat germ • 30g pinhead oatmeal
30g sesame seeds • 170g plain flour • 1 teaspoon baking soda
½ teaspoon salt • 1 teaspoon sugar • 90g butter, melted
330ml buttermilk

Method

❈ Preheat a fan oven to 190°C. Grease and dust a 1kg (2lb) loaf tin.

❈ Place all the dry ingredients in a large bowl. Using a fork, stir in the butter and buttermilk. Pour the loose bread dough into the loaf tin.

❈ Bake in the oven for 45–50 minutes. Turn off the oven. Remove the loaf from the oven and leave to stand for 10 minutes before turning out onto a rack. The loaf should sound hollow when tapped; if it doesn't, return it to the tin, turn the oven back on and bake for a further 10 minutes in the tin. For a crisper crust, return the loaf to the turned-off oven while it cools. For a softer crust, wrap the loaf in a damp tea towel while it cools.

Low-Sugar Ginger and Orange Marmalade

For as long as I can remember we have served up Mam's Brown Bread (see page 55) with home-made marmalade. I use fruit sugar to boost the sweet flavour and keep the processed sugar content down. It is naturally sweeter than sugar so the quantities needed are lower. By including ginger, you're giving the marmalade a fiery kick, which is a great counterpoint to the sweet preserve. The apple peel is important as it contains high levels of pectin, which ensures that the jam sets properly. Make sure your jars are well washed and sterilised by putting them in a low oven (140°C) for about an hour before filling them.

makes 3 jars

500g seville orange pulp with peel (blitz the whole orange in a food processor or chop it very finely – or use a prepared tin instead)

75ml freshly squeezed orange juice • 70g crystallised ginger, chopped

500g sugar • 100g fruit sugar (also known as fructose)

peel of 1 medium green apple • 225ml cold water

Method

❁ Place all the ingredients into a large saucepan and put on a medium heat. Using a wooden spoon (it's very important to use a wooden spoon as the mixture gets very hot and a metal spoon will burn your hand), stir gently until the marmalade starts to bubble. Be careful – it's hot!

❁ Turn the heat down so that you have a slow 'rolling boil', which is slightly hotter than a simmer (little bubbles) but not an intensive, hot boil. Continue stirring every 3 minutes or so and monitor the marmalade for 20 minutes. A little bit of sugar 'scum' may appear during this time. If it hasn't disappeared after the 20 minutes of a rolling boil, add a knob of butter and stir. It should disappear or, alternatively, you can scoop the scum off, but be careful as it's extremely hot!

❁ Fish out the apple peel and throw it away. Decant the marmalade into your hot sterilised jars and seal well. Wait until the jars have cooled completely before storing. If they've been properly sterilised and sealed the marmalade will keep for up to a year in a cool, dark place.

Lovely Lunches

While there are simple pleasures in a plain cheese sandwich, I can't serve them up for lunch every day. Here are some simple lunch recipes that will sustain you until your main meal. Many of the recipes in this section are portable and suitable for children's lunchboxes. And, truth be told, many of these recipes will double up as a great main meal as well.

Broccoli Soup

This is a great recipe for weaning because there are no dairy products or gluten used in the making of this soup. The garlic crisps add a crunchy texture, but you can leave these out if you are feeding a small baby or a child who's not great with strong flavours. Make this soup in advance and freeze it in small portions for easy mealtimes.

serves 6

1 tablespoon sunflower oil • 1 medium onion, peeled and roughly chopped

2 cloves of garlic, peeled and chopped

1 large head of broccoli, roughly chopped including the stalks

1 litre of hot vegetable stock or chicken stock (see page 107)

for the garlic crisps

1 tablespoon sunflower oil • 2 cloves of garlic

Method

❋ Heat a large saucepan on a medium heat.

❋ Add the sunflower oil and wait until it warms up before putting in the chopped onion. Cook, stirring regularly, until it becomes translucent.

❋ Add the garlic, stir and cook for a further 5 minutes.

❋ Gradually add the pieces of broccoli and stir until they are coated with the garlic and onion.

❋ Pour in the stock then bring to a simmer. Cut a piece of greaseproof paper into a circle slightly wider than the saucepan and fit it snugly on top of the liquid. Put the lid on the saucepan. Simmer the soup for 20 minutes.

❋ Blitz using a stick blender or mash using a potato masher.

❋ To serve with garlic crisps, fry finely sliced garlic in sunflower oil until golden brown (but not dark as it will take on a burnt flavour). For added punch, serve with slices of freshly chopped chilli with the seeds removed.

Falafel

This is a favourite street food in the Middle East. Nutty and moreish, it's best served in balls with a fresh light salad and a light dressing. The combination of chickpeas and sesame paste makes falafel high in protein and fibre. My toddler likes to grab one in each of his chubby little hands and eat them on the run. If you like coriander, just use the stalks when blending to turn the balls green and save the leaves to serve alongside your falafel.

serves 4

200g cooked chickpeas (see page 21) • 100g tahini (ground sesame paste)
2 teaspoons ginger and garlic paste (see page 14) • rind and juice of ½ lemon
handful of coriander (optional) • 2 tablespoons sunflower oil for frying

Method

※ If you have no stick blender or food processor then you can use a potato masher for this, but you get a finer result with a machine.

※ Put all the ingredients except the sunflower oil into a large bowl and mash until you have a thick pulp. Use your hands to shape into golf ball-sized lumps. Flatten a little so they take on the shape of a mini burger.

※ Take a large non-stick frying pan and heat the sunflower oil on high. Turn the heat down to medium and fry each falafel ball until golden and crispy on the outside. Serve immediately with salad and/or flatbreads (see page 64).

Flatbreads

Once you get the knack of easy flatbreads you'll be making these on a regular basis, I guarantee you. Yeast breads that you bake in the oven can be temperamental and depend on oven temperatures, but by making bread on the pan you control the temperature yourself.

makes 6 flatbreads

7g dried yeast • 1 teaspoon honey • 30ml warm (not hot) water
400g strong white flour (although plain will do too) • ½ teaspoon salt
50ml natural yoghurt

Method

🌸 Mix the yeast, honey and warm water together. Set to one side to allow the yeast to activate while you prepare the rest of the dough mixture.

🌸 Take a large bowl and put in the flour and salt. Using a fork, stir in the yoghurt until you get a breadcrumb-like texture. Pour in the activated yeast mixture and 100ml of water, then, using your hands, mix it all together and knead until you get a smooth dough. If you have a stand mixer with a dough hook it's a good idea to use it now!

🌸 Once you have a smooth dough, cover the bowl and leave to prove for approximately 90 minutes.

🌸 To cook, take a dry, non-stick frying pan and heat on medium. Take a piece of the dough about the size of the palm of your hand and flatten it out before placing the dough on the pan to cook. Alternatively, take small ping-pong ball-sized pieces and cook smaller rounds instead.

🌸 Turn when it is brown underneath. Keep all the flatbreads warm in the oven before serving with dips, falafel curry, chilli or anything that needs mopping or wrapping!

Broad-Bean Pesto

While broad beans make a great pesto, you can also make this recipe with peas. Spread it on toast, toss it through pasta or stir it into a bit of scrambled egg to mix up how you serve it.

serves 5

150g broad beans, shelled • 3 cloves of garlic • 1 handful of fresh coriander
olive oil • lemon juice

Method

❀ Put the broad beans into a large jug, peel and roughly chop the garlic and add it to the jug.

❀ Rip the coriander and add to the jug as well.

❀ Put a glug of olive oil on top and use a stick blender to pulse to a paste.

❀ Squeeze the juice of half a lemon on top and pulse again.

❀ Season to taste.

Tabbouleh

The first time I ate this salad I was sitting in a hot, dusty restaurant in the south of Lebanon. Time spent in the Middle East as a child changed my tastes forever.

I've never been able to find a restaurant or person who can replicate the right flavour. Most people seem to add loads of couscous to tabbouleh. In our house we use a little bulgar wheat and leave the salad to ferment a little overnight, then dress the following day and serve. I've put the ingredients in cup measures as that's how it works best. One cup is equivalent to about 250ml in a measuring jug.

serves 4

1 cup parsley • ½ cup mint • 3 fresh tomatoes
½ white onion (it must be white) • 1 teaspoon salt (I know it sounds like a lot but it aids the fermentation process) • ½ cup bulgar wheat • ½ cup hot water
¼ cup lemon juice • ¼ cup olive oil

Method

❁ Chop the parsley and mint finely. Tumble into a large bowl.

❁ Halve the tomatoes and scoop out the seeds. You can use these later in a tomato sauce, so freeze them if you're not going to use them immediately. Cut the tomatoes finely and add to the bowl.

❁ Peel and chop the onion (if you want to save time you can grate it using a coarse grater straight into the bowl). Pour in the salt and stir well.

❁ Take a cereal bowl, pour in the bulgar wheat and cover with hot water. Leave to sit for 20 minutes. Strain off any excess water and add the bulgar wheat into the salad ingredients. It will not be completely cooked at this stage but the fermentation process overnight aids the cooking and the bulgar wheat will soak up any juices that come out of the vegetables.

❁ To serve, mix the fresh lemon juice and olive oil together, then pour over the salad. Eat with freshly toasted pitta bread or flat bread.

Minestrone

You can add cooked beans towards the end of making this minestrone, but it's not essential and we often eat it without the addition. This soup is still highly nutritious and full of antioxidants.

serves 4 for lunch or 2 for dinner

1 onion, peeled and chopped • 1 tablespoon olive oil
1 clove of garlic, peeled and chopped • 2 carrots, peeled and chopped
2 peppers, cored and chopped • 400g tin of chopped tomatoes • 100g pasta
100g cooked beans (optional)

Method

❄ In a large saucepan on a medium heat, cook the onion in the olive oil for 10 minutes before adding the garlic. Cook for a further 5 minutes then add the carrots and peppers. Stir well and allow to heat through, then pour in the tomatoes from the tin. Fill the empty tin with water and pour into the pot.

❄ Cover and simmer for 90 minutes. Stir occasionally and keep an eye on the water level. Add a little extra water (about 100ml) then pour in the pasta to cook in the soup mixture itself. Pour in the beans at this stage if you are using them.

❄ Simmer the soup for a further 15 minutes before serving and allow everybody to season to their own taste at the table.

Mixed Salad

When food is fresh and plentiful there is a great sense of generosity in serving up plenty of what you know the family will eat and letting everyone serve themselves from the bowl. If you grow some of your own vegetables you can have salad all through the summer for practically nothing. Feel free to mix and match the ingredients here: this is merely a starting point to send you in the right direction.

A great trick to making a salad last a little longer is to dress it on the plate, rather than in the bowl. That way, any salad you don't eat will keep in a sealed container in the fridge for a further 24 hours.

Unless serving straight away, cut softer vegetables first and put them at the bottom of the bowl, then drier ones on top. This will prevent green leaves, such as lettuce or herbs, from getting soggy while waiting to be eaten.

serves 4

4 ripe tomatoes or 250g cherry tomatoes • ½ cucumber
1 medium white onion or 6 spring onions, peeled • 1 red/yellow pepper
½ head of lettuce or 4 handfuls of fresh leaves • honey and mustard dressing (see page 201) • 1 handful of mixed nuts or 4 hard boiled eggs (optional)

Method

❋ Cut the tomatoes into bite-sized chunks and place in the bottom of a large salad bowl. Slice the cucumber in half lengthways and use a teaspoon to scoop out and discard the seeds (you can leave these in if you like but they can make the salad very watery). Cut the cucumber into bite-sized chunks and pop on top of the tomatoes.

❋ Peel and slice the onion into tiny pieces. Don't do bite-sized here as you may end up burning your mouth when eating the raw onion. If you don't like raw onion, consider adding 2 tablespoons of my spiced onion mixture (see page 202) instead.

❋ Cut the top off the pepper and remove the core, then chop into bite-sized pieces and add to the salad bowl.

❋ Wash the lettuce if necessary, dry on a piece of kitchen paper and put on top of the other salad components.

❋ Finally, serve with the salad dressing for everyone to add to their own plate.

❋ To make this mixed salad a main meal, include the nuts or eggs, which will add protein, and serve with crusty bread or steamed potatoes.

Hummus

Kids love the mild flavours and soft texture in hummus, so it makes a great weaning option. For adults you can stir in freshly squeezed lemon juice, some dried chilli powder and some garlic purée for an extra punch.

I cut the vegetables for the dip into chunky pieces, suitable for chubby hands to grasp and chew on. When my toddler was a baby he loved the peppery flavour of whole spring onions and the cooling texture of cucumber. He still eats chickpeas like sweets so I always tumble a couple onto the side of the plate for him.

You can eat hummus straightaway, but I prefer to make it a day or so before eating, to allow the flavours to mature. A vegetable masher will do in a pinch but a stick blender or food processor gives the best results. For a very smooth texture you will need to squeeze each chickpea out of its skin individually, but I leave the skins on as I prefer to keep the fibre.

serves 4

300g cooked chickpeas (see page 21) • 3 cloves of garlic, peeled and crushed
100g tahini (ground sesame paste) • 100ml olive oil • rind and juice of 1 lemon
chopped vegetables to serve

Method

✿ Blitz the chickpeas and garlic together.

✿ Add the tahini, olive oil and lemon juice and rind and blitz again. If it's a bit too thick, add a little warm water until you get the texture you like.

✿ Season to taste.

✿ Serve with flatbreads (see page 64) and/or a selection of vegetables cut into a suitable shape for dipping, e.g. carrot sticks, chunks of celery, strips of pepper or small florets of broccoli or cauliflower.

Family Salad Jar

A salad that is suitable for picnics or parties alike. It doesn't really take an awful lot of preparation but it sits in the fridge until I'm ready to serve. If I'm making a pasta dish, I'll just make double quantities and keep the extra in the fridge, tossed in a little olive oil to stop it sticking, for use in this recipe. A cup is equivalent to the 250ml mark in a measuring jug.

serves 4

4 tablespoons olive oil • 2 tablespoons cider vinegar • 200g cooked pasta
3 medium carrots • 1 cup frozen peas • 1 cup frozen sweetcorn
1 medium cucumber • 4 boiled eggs

Method

❀ Take a large jar (I use a 2-litre volume kilner-style jar) and pour the oil, vinegar and some seasoning in the bottom. Tumble the pasta in on top.

❀ Peel and finely chop the carrots, pour on top. Pour the frozen peas on top, as they are, followed by the sweetcorn. Chop the cucumber in half lengthways, and use a teaspoon to scoop out the seeds and throw them in the bin. Chop the cucumber into chunks and pour on top of the other vegetables.

❀ Peel and chop the eggs into quarters and add to the jar.

❀ Seal the jar and refrigerate until ready to eat. This salad will keep for up to two days in the fridge. Shake before serving to distribute the dressing.

Raspberry Ricotta Scones

Easy to make and eat, scones are a firm family favourite for lunchtimes. The tart raspberries and sweet ricotta make for a sweet scone. A real treat, I serve these scones up with a variety of chopped fruit such as apples, pears and bananas, to balance lunch.

makes 12 medium-sized scones

250g plain flour • 1 teaspoon baking soda • 75g ricotta • 1 tablespoon honey
50ml buttermilk • 100g frozen raspberries

Method

✿ Preheat a fan oven to 200°C. Line a baking tray with greaseproof paper and dust with flour.

✿ Weigh out the flour and baking soda into a large bowl. Using a fork, mix in the ricotta and honey, then pour in the buttermilk and mix again.

✿ Mix in the raspberries. You'll get a stiff dough. Try not to work it too much.

✿ Transfer the dough onto a clean board dusted with flour, flatten it to about 2cm and cut out the scones. Transfer the scones to the baking tray.

✿ Bake in the oven for 20–25 minutes, cool for a few minutes on a wire rack and serve with butter and jam.

Sesame Crackers

We love crackers in my house, where they serve as both a tasty snack and a baby weaning tool! They are so easy to make, I just take a portion off my pizza dough when I'm getting ready to make pizza and roll out the cracker shapes. The boys love cutting the crackers into fun shapes and munching on them when they're still warm.

serves 4 for lunch

¼ quantity of pizza dough (see page 187) • 100g sesame seeds
flour for sprinkling

to serve

cheese and sliced tomato or hummus (see page 74)
or tabbouleh (see page 69)

Method

❀ Preheat a fan oven to 210°C and line a baking tray with greaseproof paper.

❀ Sprinkle a clean, flat surface with flour. Roll out the dough as flat as you can get it. Sprinkle the sesame seeds on top and roll again so that they are embedded into the dough.

❀ Cut the dough into shapes and place on the lined baking tray. Bake in the oven until golden brown. The time it takes will depend on how thinly you roll your dough. Make sure your oven light is on and watch the baking tray closely. Mine take about 7 minutes to bake.

❀ Cool on a wire rack and then serve with your chosen topping.

❀ The crackers will keep in a dry airtight container for up to three days.

Tuna Melt

One small tin of tuna will go a long way in this house. I bulk it up with lots of fresh vegetables and a small sprinkling of cheese.

serves 5

10 slices of bread • 127g tin of tuna in brine • 1 red pepper
1 yellow pepper • 3 spring onions • 2 tablespoons mayonnaise
50g grated cheese

Method

❀ Toast the bread.

❀ Strain the tuna and place in a large bowl. Use a fork to crumble the pieces.

❀ Chop the peppers and onions into small pieces and stir into the tuna.

❀ Add the mayonnaise and stir well until every piece is coated.

❀ Divide the tuna mixture between each slice of toast and give the top a very light sprinkling of cheese.

❀ Grill until golden brown on top.

Fifteen-Minute Suppers

Just fifteen minutes — that is all it takes to make one of these swift suppers? That's quicker than the wait for a takeaway delivery or for a frozen pizza to cook in the oven. If you slot just one of my supper recipes into your weekly meal plans instead of eating convenience food, you'll save yourself money, time and stress.

Bread Pesto Quesadillas

I know that it may be a stretch of the imagination to call this recipe a classic 'pesto', but the main flavours of pesto are basil and garlic. I use up leftover bread to make bread pesto and spread it on a wrap. Add cheese and you have a great quesadilla. You will need a small electric chopper or stick blender for this recipe. You could, at a stretch, chop everything finely and mix, but this gets a finer blend. You could also stir it through pasta or use it in any of the ways you might use any other pesto.

fills a 300g jar

3 slices stale bread (brown sliced pan works best here)

3 handfuls of fresh basil (leaves and stalks are okay as it will get pulsed)

5 cloves of garlic, peeled • 75ml olive oil

to serve

2 tortilla wraps per portion • 1 tablespoon bread pesto per portion

30g cheese per portion

Method

❊ Blitz all the pesto ingredients together and decant into a resealable jam jar. This pesto will keep in the fridge for over a week, covered in a thin layer of olive oil.

❊ Heat a non-stick frying pan on a medium heat.

❊ Take one wrap and place it in the dry frying pan. Grate cheese on top. Take a second wrap and spread it with a tablespoon of the pesto mixture. After 3 minutes put the pesto wrap face down on top of the cheese and flip carefully using a spatula.

❊ Heat on the frying pan for a further 5 minutes until golden brown and crispy.

❊ Slice into triangles and serve with a green salad, fresh cut tomatoes and chopped cucumber.

Quick Soup

When you are looking for a fragrant soup in a hurry, this is far better for you than pre-prepared dehydrated packets. I keep a jar of minced ginger and garlic in the fridge: it costs me €1.49 in my local grocery shop but I know it can be bought for even less in Asian food stores. Warming just one teaspoon of this mixture fills the house with a wonderful smell. You can, of course, mince it yourself, but this is a huge time saver.

serves 1

1 teaspoon ginger and garlic paste (see page 14) • 1 teaspoon soy sauce
1 teaspoon sesame oil • 200ml hot water or, better, hot chicken stock (see page 107) 1 small carrot, peeled and finely sliced • 1 spring onion, finely sliced
2 teaspoons frozen sweetcorn • 2 teaspoons frozen peas
1 chilli, finely sliced (optional) • a handful of fine rice noodles (optional)

Method

❊ Take a large bowl and put the ginger and garlic paste, soy sauce and sesame oil in the bottom. Pour over the hot water/stock. Toss in the vegetables (including the chilli if you're using it) and stir.

❊ If you want a hearty, filling meal then add some fine rice noodles to the bowl before serving.

Spring Ricepaper Rolls

When I have fresh ingredients I believe in making the most of them and rarely cook what I can eat raw. I use ricepaper wrappers to make my rolls, but if you're stuck you can just as easily use lettuce or cabbage leaves; the trick here is to wrap them tightly.

serves 4

for the dipping sauce

50ml soy sauce • 1 chilli, finely sliced • 1 clove of garlic, finely sliced
1 piece of ginger (the same size as the clove of garlic), finely sliced

for the rolls

2 carrots, peeled • 1 handful of radishes • 3 spring onions, topped and tailed
4 ricepaper wrappers

Method

✿ Take a small dish and mix together all the ingredients for the dipping sauce. Cover and leave to one side.

✿ Chop each of the fresh vegetables into fine slices of equal length where possible.

✿ Boil a kettle of water. Take a large dinner plate and pour a little of the hot water onto the plate. Be careful! Quickly dip a ricepaper wrapper into the water. It will soften a little but not totally. That's great because it makes it easier to work with.

✿ Move the wrapper to a clean, smooth surface/chopping board.

✿ Pile a quarter of the fresh chopped vegetables in the middle of the wrapper. Fold in three sides, leaving one free. Tightly roll the wrapper towards the free end. Compact hard as you roll. Use a little water on your finger to seal the wrapper when you reach the end.

✿ Cut in half before serving with the dipping sauce.

Warm Salmon Salad

Yes, I know smoked salmon is expensive, particularly around Christmas. However, in the summer you'll often find it on special offer. This recipe makes a little go a long way and the green leaves add loads of nutrients. If you're stuck for time, use cold cooked potatoes from a meal the night before. It's always a good idea to plan ahead for quick lunches and if you're boiling/steaming a pot of potatoes, a few extra will save you time the following day.

serves 5

2 tablespoons sunflower oil

5 medium potatoes, peeled (or cooked potatoes from the previous night)

10 leaves young chard • 1 handful of young spinach • 70g smoked salmon

squeeze of fresh lemon juice

Method

❋ Put a non-stick frying pan on a medium heat and add the sunflower oil. Finely slice the potatoes lengthways about 1cm thick and fry them in the oil until golden brown. Drain on some kitchen paper to get rid of the excess oil.

❋ Meanwhile, tear the chard and spinach into bite-sized pieces. Slice the salmon into long strips and toss together with the leaves.

❋ Serve with the potatoes at the bottom, then tumble the salmon and green leaves on top of the hot potatoes. Squeeze fresh lemon juice on top – the salmon is oily enough that this is all the dressing you need. Eat before the green leaves wilt too much.

Loaded Nachos

Perfect Saturday night food and a great way to get rid of any leftover vegetables in your fridge. If you don't like salted corn nachos, then consider slicing and baking some tortilla wraps until crispy.

serves 4

2 packets of ready salted nachos • shredded leftover chicken pieces
1 or 2 peppers, cored and finely sliced • 75g frozen sweetcorn
1 small onion, peeled and finely sliced (or a large spring onion)
3 tomatoes, chopped and seeded • 1 chilli, finely sliced (optional)
1 ball of budget mozzarella or some grated cheese
sour cream or cream cheese to serve

Method

❀ Preheat a fan oven to 180°C.

❀ Pour the nachos into a baking tray or two, then sprinkle all the other ingredients on top. (We normally make two trays: one for the kids without spicy stuff, and one for us with some finely sliced chilli and fresh herbs like basil on top as well.)

❀ Bake in the oven for 15 minutes, then bring the baking trays to the table and spoon onto plates. Serve with some cream cheese or sour cream.

Fried Rice

If there ever was a reason to keep lots of fresh vegetables in the house along with frozen, then fried rice is it. There are plenty of time-saving tricks to make this work for you!

Whenever you're cooking a dish with rice, make twice as much as you need. Allow the leftover rice to cool, spread out on a tray. Then, once cold, scoop into a freezer bag and stick straight in the freezer.

I've used American cup measurements here as it's a loose recipe you can adjust to your own taste and what you have in the house. A cup is equivalent to about 250ml in a measuring jug.

For a quick, wholesome meal all you need to do is assemble this dish, which can be topped with a fried egg if you like. For us, it's a meal in itself.

serves 5

2 tablespoons sunflower oil • 3 cups cooked rice (defrosted if frozen)
1 teaspoon ginger and garlic paste (see page 14) • 1 teaspoon five-spice mix
1 cup frozen peas • 1 cup frozen sweetcorn • 1 small head of broccoli, cut into florets
3 carrots, peeled and sliced • 5 spring onions, peeled and chopped
soy sauce to taste

Method

❄ Heat a wok or a very large non-stick saucepan over a high heat. Add the sunflower oil. Add in the cooked rice and allow it to sizzle for a minute or two.

❄ Spoon the paste and five-spice mix on top, then stir around the cooked rice. Pour the peas, sweetcorn, broccoli and carrots on top.

❄ Cover and allow the vegetables to steam in their own juices for 5 minutes. The rice will get a bit sticky and caramelised on the bottom. Don't worry, it's meant to as it adds to the flavour and texture. If you feel it is burning or the saucepan is too hot, then turn the temperature down a little at this stage.

❄ Remove the lid and stir again. Add the chopped spring onions, stir once more and serve sprinkled with the soy sauce.

Gigot Chop with Warm Broad-Bean Salad

I always associate gigot chop with traditional Irish stew, but if you have a decent chop you can either remove the bones yourself or ask your butcher to do it for you. A simple marinade and a hot, searing pan will result in a moist piece of lamb that is a hit with everyone.

serves 5

3 tablespoons sunflower oil • 1 teaspoon garlic powder • 1 teaspoon paprika
3 gigot lamb chops • 1 head of cauliflower • 70g broad beans
1 yellow pepper • 1 tablespoon balsamic vinegar • 1 stale Vienna loaf

Method

❀ Combine the oil, garlic powder, paprika and a pinch of salt and pepper, and marinade the lamb in this mixture for at least 1 hour.

❀ Heat a griddle pan on high. Slice the cauliflower into broad slices about 1cm thick. Pod the broad beans (if they haven't already been done). Chop the yellow pepper into pieces the same size as the beans.

❀ Take the lamb out of the marinade and leave the marinade aside. Cook the lamb on the griddle for about 7 minutes each side, then remove and leave to rest.

❀ Dip the cauliflower in the reserved marinade and put on the griddle. Cook on both sides, then remove and leave to rest. Sprinkle the broad beans and pepper on the griddle, followed by the vinegar. Turn the heat off and scoop the beans and pepper to the edges of the griddle pan. Toast slices of the bread in the juices left behind.

❀ Once rested, the lamb will slice easily – remove any hard pieces of gristle or sinew before serving. Start with the toast on the bottom, then the cauliflower, beans and pepper, then finally the lamb. Drizzle with any juices left in the pan.

Take One Chicken, Make Many Meals

The beauty of roast chicken is that you will definitely get three meals from a medium-sized bird. Chicken is one of the more frugal protein sources. I talk about it so much when I'm telling people about how to eke more than one meal out of a cut of meat that my hubby has been known to tell me that he can't face any for a week?

Roast Chicken

I used to roast a chicken, pick the two breasts off and then discard the rest. Oh my goodness, the sheer waste of it now turns my stomach!

If you're looking for a fabulous recipe to flavour the chicken then look away now, because I don't flavour the chicken at the roasting stage apart from a little salt, pepper and butter wrappers. The reason for this is I want to use the leftover meat and then also make stock from the carcass. If I were to use lots of lemon or flavoured herbs when roasting the bird, I would end up with an awful stock. Instead I add a flavoured butter at the end when serving the chicken.

serves 4 for 2 dinners ✿
and makes 1 batch of chicken stock for a third dinner

1 medium chicken (about 1.5kg) • 3 butter wrappers

for the herb butter (optional)

fresh herbs – whatever is available • 50g butter, softened

Method

✿ My tips and tricks for a perfect roast chicken involve using leftover butter wrappers – I don't throw anything away when I don't have to! Butter wrappers are perfect because they have little bits of butter still stuck on them and they have double insulation from the greaseproof wrapper and the tinfoil. Three of these wrappers should cover a medium bird. If you don't have a wrapper, then spread butter on a large piece of greaseproof paper, place it buttered side down on the bird and then put tinfoil on top, shiny side facing inwards.

✿ Preheat the oven to 160°C. I use a standard grill pan, sit my chicken on the rack and fill an inch or so of water into the pan underneath. This keeps the chicken moist from below. Roast for the amount of time you need, depending on the weight of the bird. I know that sounds a bit imprecise, but your butcher will tell you how much it weighs and how long you need to cook it for. Mine normally take 90 minutes at 160°C, then a further 10 minutes at 200°C with the wrapper off to get a golden brown colour.

✿ Once the chicken is cooked, take it out of the oven and wrap it well with tinfoil (or put the butter wrappers back on) and allow it to rest for at least 30 minutes before carving.

✿ If you fancy herbs with your chicken add them at this stage so that the fresh flavour of the garden shines through. Sage goes fantastically with chicken. Chop a handful of sage leaves into small pieces (but not too fine as they will lose their flavour). Mash into the softened butter then spread on top of the warm roast chicken. The butter will melt in the heat and it will release the sage aroma.

Real Gravy

Once you try real gravy and get it right you'll be making it every time you have a roast. We never used any of the instant gravies when we were growing up. They are full of salt and don't really taste of meat.

Why not make your own? You have all the ingredients to hand and you won't believe how easy it is! This recipe is for chicken gravy, but the principle is the same no matter what cut of meat you've roasted. You should get 300–500ml of gravy.

ingredients

1 roast chicken (or beef or pork) • 30g plain flour

Method

- Lift the roast meat off the rack and put on a plate to rest, covered with tinfoil. Put the rack in the sink for cleaning later.
- Remember you used a small amount of water in the roasting tray to keep the chicken moist? There should be some of this water left. If not, splash about 100ml of boiling water or chicken stock (see page 107) into the tray to loosen the cooking juices. Using a wooden spoon, scrape the bottom of the roasting tin until you get all the juices and crusty bits in a pile, then pour into a small saucepan. Heat the saucepan on medium until the liquid is bubbling. Season with a pinch of salt and pepper.
- Sprinkle in the flour and boil a kettle. Stir the mixture in the saucepan until it starts to bubble. Carefully add a splash of hot water and stir well again. Continue to add splashes of water and stir until you get the gravy to the thickness you want.
- At this stage, taste the gravy. Adjust the seasoning if you need to, then serve.

Chicken Stock

I often see jars or cartons of chicken stock in the supermarket and I cannot get over the price that you have to pay for it when the real deal is so cheap and easy to make at home. I guess there is always going to be a price for convenience. There is nothing like the smell of chicken stock bubbling on the hob. It fills the house and makes us all feel amazing. It is one of those smells, just like baking bread, that brings a smile to your face.

The key to making good stock isn't to do with the flavourings you use, far from it. Chicken stock should be pure, without any other flavouring.

Once you've had a lovely roast chicken meal (see page 103) and used up the leftover meat for another meal, you're left with a carcass. If you like you can freeze the carcass and wait until you have three at once to make a large batch of stock. I prefer to have fresh stock on the go once a week.

Method

❋ Take the picked-over carcass and using either your hands or a sharp knife, split it into about 4 pieces. Splitting the pieces isn't essential, but it helps to lower the cooking time and increase the surface area for caramelisation and, therefore, flavour. Put the carcass on a baking tray lined with tinfoil and roast in the oven for 20 minutes at 200°C.

❋ Boil a kettle and grab a big saucepan with a lid. Tumble the roasted bones into the large saucepan, cover with hot water and put on a low heat. It should immediately start to simmer. Cover the pot, then leave to simmer for 60 minutes.

❋ While still warm, strain away the bones and decant the liquid into a sealed, sterilised jar and allow to cool before refrigerating.

❋ Home-made stock will keep in the fridge for up to two days or in the freezer for a couple of months.

Chicken Soup

When I have a whole chicken one of my first instincts is to roast it. However, by immersing the whole bird in water you'll get an intense flavoured broth, which becomes a soup, while the meat remains succulent and moist for use in other recipes.

serves 4

1 medium chicken (about 1.5kg) • 1 onion, cut into chunks
4 carrots, peeled and chopped • 1 turnip, peeled and chopped
1 handful of fresh mangetout, chopped

Method

❉ Remove any strings or plastic ties from the chicken. Put the chicken in a large pot and cover with 2.5 litres of cold water. Pop in the onion. Bring to a slow simmer.

❉ Simmer gently for 90 minutes.

❉ Toss in the carrot and turnip. Simmer for a further 15 minutes.

❉ Tumble in the mangetout. All you want is to heat it through as it's nicest crispy and green.

❉ Ladle the stock and vegetables into a dish (it's easier to ladle off the stock and vegetables first), then remove the chicken carefully using tongs and tear some of the breast for the soup. Cover the remaining chicken for use for another meal.

❉ Serve immediately with steamed potatoes or crusty bread.

Creamy Chicken Bake

So you've roasted or poached a chicken and used some of it for your dinner, but what do you do with the rest? This creamy chicken bake is deliciously easy and quick to make. It is great with any carbohydrates, but I prefer it with plain pasta or rice.

serves 3 adults and 2 children

30g butter • 30g plain flour • 200ml hot milk (I heat it in the microwave)

200ml hot water or chicken stock (see page 107)

grating of nutmeg • 2 whole carrots, peeled

chicken meat from the picked-over carcass of a cooked chicken

2 red peppers, cored and sliced • 50g rolled oats

Method

❀ Preheat a fan oven to 180°C.

❀ Melt the butter in a large saucepan on a medium heat and sprinkle in the flour. Cook for 3 minutes, then bit by bit add the hot milk, stirring every time. The sauce will get very thick. Once the milk is gone start adding the water/stock bit by bit.

❀ Add some salt, pepper and a grating of nutmeg. Grate in the carrots using the coarse side of the grater. Stir in the chicken and let all the ingredients get warm.

❀ Pour the sauce into a large baking tray, pop the sliced peppers on top and sprinkle over the oats. Bake in the oven for 30 minutes before serving with pasta or rice.

Shakin' Chicken Nuggets (Gluten Free)

When making the chicken soup (see page 108), consider removing the breasts from the chicken before cooking to make these tasty, gluten-free nuggets. If you're a bit squeamish, ask your butcher to do this for you – he will be happy to do it.

The use of gram (chickpea) flour in this recipe keeps the nuggets gluten free, which makes them lighter and easier to digest. It also adds a mild nutty flavour to the coating and my kids love them. It's another way to sneak some fibre into their diet, particularly for picky kids who normally won't eat anything different unless you disguise it.

serves 4

2 whole chicken fillets • 200ml buttermilk • 2 cloves of garlic
1 tablespoon sunflower oil • 100g gram (chickpea) flour
pinch each of salt, cracked black pepper, paprika, cumin, coriander and garlic powder

Method

❊ Slice the chicken fillets into thin strips, put into a large bowl and cover with the buttermilk. Crush the garlic into the bowl and stir. Cover with cling film and chill for at least 1 hour.

❊ Lightly oil a non-stick frying pan and bring to a medium heat.

❊ Pour the remaining ingredients into a large freezer bag, seal and shake. Strain the chicken from the buttermilk, discard the milk and garlic. Put the chicken into the bag with the dry ingredients, seal and shake well until each piece is well coated.

❊ Fry in batches of five or six, so as not to cram the pan, until golden on each side. Serve with dips such as tomato relish (see page 206) or hummus (see page 74) and fresh vegetable batons.

Moroccan Chicken with Couscous

After one roast chicken or poached chicken dinner it's easy to spice up the leftovers so that you don't get caught up eating bland food. This meal takes 20 minutes to make from start to finish.

serves 6

100g mangetout, sliced • 100g frozen sweetcorn
1 teaspoon butter • 1 teaspoon sunflower oil
½ teaspoon each of ground cumin, coriander, ginger, cinnamon and paprika
200g dried couscous • 3 handfuls of cooked chicken pieces
1 handful of sultanas or raisins • 1 handful of dried apricots
fresh vegetables, diced – e.g. peppers, cucumbers, tomatoes (optional)

Method

❀ Put the kettle on to boil. Weigh out the frozen vegetables and put to one side.

❀ Melt the butter in the oil in a frying pan on a low heat. Pour in the ground spices and cook them until their aroma is released.

❀ Put the couscous in a large cereal bowl, as it will expand to at least double its volume. Pour hot water over the couscous until it is just about 2cm above the dried couscous. Stir with a fork, cover with a plate and leave it to soak.

❀ Add the chicken and dried fruit to the frying pan. Toss until heated through.

❀ Uncover the couscous and stir in the sweetcorn, peas and any other fresh vegetables you like.

❀ Serve the chicken over the couscous in a large serving dish in the middle of the table.

Quick Chicken Pie

I love dinners that require little preparation and mess. When I make my roast chicken (see page 103), I make lashings of real gravy (see page 104) so I know there will be plenty left over. I know that this pie will be a real treat for the family and that it is very quick and easy to assemble. We jokingly refer to this as our 'coleslaw' pie because of the carrot and cabbage in the filling.

serves 6

3 handfuls of leftover roast chicken • 250ml leftover gravy
2 carrots, peeled • half a medium green or white cabbage
8 medium potatoes, peeled • 30g butter, melted

Method

❋ Preheat a fan oven to 180°C.

❋ Put the chicken in a large mixing bowl, pour over the leftover gravy. Grate in the carrots using a coarse grade.

❋ Finely shred or slice the cabbage and add it to the bowl. Stir well and pour the whole mixture into a large baking dish. The cabbage and carrot have some water content so don't be too stressed if the mixture appears quite thick at this stage – it will become more liquid as the pie heats, as will the gravy.

❋ Slice the potatoes lengthways to about 1cm thick and cover the top of the pie with the sliced potatoes, overlapping as necessary. Brush with melted butter and bake in the oven for 1 hour.

Chicken Korma

This sauce is amazing. It is so fragrant and full of spice yet not too hot on the tongue. I love using it on leftover chicken, but it's great with any meat or just vegetables. The key is to make loads of the sauce in advance because it needs to cook slowly. Once cooked and cooled you can freeze the sauce in portions for a quick meal any time of the day or night.

serves 4

1 teaspoon coriander seeds • 1 teaspoon cumin seeds

1 whole clove • ½ teaspoon dried chilli • 1 teaspoon turmeric

2 teaspoons ginger and garlic paste (see page 14) • 1 tablespoon sunflower oil

1 onion, finely chopped • 400g tin of chopped tomatoes

100ml coconut milk (or more if you prefer a creamier sauce)

3 handfuls of cooked chicken and/or other main ingredients

2 tablespoons fish sauce

Method

❋ Heat the coriander, cumin, clove and chilli until fragrant on a dry non-stick frying pan. Be careful – the chilli will make you cough if you inhale too near the pan! Once toasted, pour the spices into a mortar and pestle, then grind well with the turmeric.

❋ Return the pan to the heat and pour in the ginger and garlic paste, the sunflower oil and the onion. Sizzle gently for about 10 minutes, pour in the ground dried spices and allow to infuse for another 5 minutes.

❋ Add the chopped tomatoes, stir then add the coconut milk (you can get small tins in the supermarket but you can also use a bigger tin here if you like).

❋ Cover and simmer the sauce for 1 hour before adding meat and/or vegetables of your choice.

❋ Heat through and then season using the fish sauce and some black pepper.

Chicken Stuffing Bake

One of the reasons why I never cook stuffing in a chicken is because I don't like to mess with the flavour of the inevitable stock (see page 107).

There's nothing stopping me from using it to make a beautiful crumble-topped bake though! The trick when making this is to prepare in advance for less effort later. So, when making a roast chicken dinner, cook double quantities of all the vegetables (including potatoes) and the gravy.

serves 4

50g butter • 1 onion, finely chopped • 1 handful of fresh parsley, finely chopped
100g breadcrumbs • 3 handfuls of leftover roast chicken • 250ml leftover gravy
cooked vegetables of choice – leftover if available, or cooked fresh. I use
cauliflower, broccoli, peas, turnip, carrots, potatoes – whatever is to hand.

Method

* Melt the butter on a medium heat in a large frying pan. Cook the chopped onions in the melted butter until translucent (this will take about 10 minutes). Stir in the fresh parsley and the breadcrumbs. Toast the breadcrumbs in the pan for about 5 minutes. Remove from the heat.

* Preheat a fan oven to 170°C.

* Take a large baking dish and pour in the roast chicken, gravy and cooked vegetables. Stir together. Sprinkle the breadcrumb mixture on top.

* Bake in the oven for 25 minutes, then serve.

Chicken Caesar Salad

Caesar salad is traditionally made with romaine lettuce, an anchovy sauce and very rarely includes chicken. However, this is a more modern take on the salad. The kids love helping me with the preparation of this dish and, importantly, it includes leftover chicken from a roast.

serves 4

2 carrots, peeled • 3 handfuls of cherry tomatoes
150g fresh green leaves (I like rocket) • 5 chives
3 tablespoons mayonnaise • 1 teaspoon garlic powder
juice of half a lemon • 3–4 handfuls of leftover roast chicken

Method

❋ Take a large bowl and shred the prepared carrots into it with a vegetable peeler, so that you get long ribbons. Wash and dry the tomatoes before adding them into the bowl along with the washed and dried green leaves.

❋ Finely chop the chives, put half into the large bowl and the other half into a smaller bowl for the dressing.

❋ Add the mayonnaise, garlic powder, lemon juice and some cracked black pepper to the chives in the small bowl. Stir with a fork until you get a loose dressing.

❋ Divide the salad between four plates, tumble the chicken on top and drizzle with the lemon and garlic dressing. Serve with crusty bread.

Quick Chicken Satay

You could spend an awful lot of time trying to replicate an original satay sauce at home or you could cheat. I'm all for saving time and money. The key to this sauce is to get a decent quality, flavoursome chunky peanut butter.

serves 4 🍁

2 chicken breasts • 200ml whole milk
1 teaspoon ginger and garlic paste (see page 14)
1 teaspoon paprika • 150g crunchy peanut butter
50g sweet chilli sauce • 2 tablespoons soy sauce

Method

❄ Take twenty wooden skewers and soak them in water in a long tray or dish.

❄ Slice the chicken breasts lengthways as thinly as you can, bearing in mind they will have to sit on skewers so not paper-thin! You should get about four to five pieces from one chicken breast. Each piece will sit individually lengthways on a skewer.

❄ Put the milk, ginger and garlic paste and paprika into a jug or bowl. Stir well, then put the raw chicken into the mixture. Cover and chill in the fridge for at least 1 hour, but no more than 4 hours as the chicken will become too tender and won't stick to the skewers.

❄ Mix the peanut butter, sweet chilli sauce and soy sauce together in a small bowl. I don't heat the satay sauce, as the peanut butter tends to clump when you heat and mix it. If you feel it's not runny enough, add a little water or more soy sauce. Taste as you go.

❄ After the chicken has marinaded, strain off the liquid and skewer each piece carefully. Cook on a barbecue, under the grill or on a griddle pan. On a hot pan or barbecue the chicken will take 7 minutes to cook – 3½ minutes on each side.

❄ Serve with the satay sauce as a dip or drizzle it over the hot chicken. Serve with boiled or steamed rice and a fresh salad, such as lettuce, tomatoes, onions – whatever is in season. Cut raw vegetables into batons or chunks so that you can scoop up any leftover satay sauce.

ESP:
Eggs, Spuds and Pulses

These are my three magic ingredients? We all need a little bit of E (eggs), S (spuds or potatoes) and P (pulses or beans) to get us through the week. As alternative protein sources to meat, eggs and pulses save me a fortune, and the pulses and spuds are full of fibre as well. These form a significant part of my larder staples.

Cowboy Beans

Baked beans with horns on! If you're looking for a plain tomato baked beans recipe then you're on the wrong page. These beans have a kick and use up the crunchy bits left over when you're making a roast, although a few rashers of bacon as an alternative is fine. If you're catering for a vegan, then leave all sources of meat and dairy protein out. As with most of my bean recipes, I like to make a big batch of the cowboy beans.

serves 6 hungry cowboys or girls

100g dried butterbeans • 1 tablespoon sunflower oil

1 large onion, peeled and chopped • 2 cloves of garlic, peeled and chopped

4 stalks of celery, chopped • 4 carrots, peeled and chopped

400g tin of chopped tomatoes • 1 tablespoon Tabasco sauce

1 tablespoon Worcester sauce

50g crispy roasted meat or 5 rashers of bacon cooked and chopped

Method

✻ The day before you are cooking this recipe put the butter beans into a large bowl with 300ml of cold water to soak. Make sure you leave plenty of room for expansion!

✻ Heat the sunflower oil in a large saucepan over a medium heat. Fry the chopped onion and garlic until almost see-through/translucent. This takes about 10 minutes. Add the celery and carrots and fry for a further 10 minutes.

✻ Pour in the tomatoes and 500ml of water, mix well, then add the Tabasco and Worcester sauces. Tumble in the beans with any leftover water from soaking, stir and cover the saucepan. Bring to a gentle simmer and leave simmering on the hob for 90 minutes.

✻ Stir every now and again, keep an eye on the water content and if it seems a little dry add some more hot water to the pot. The beans soak up a lot.

✻ Before serving stir in the crispy meat. This is a meal in itself, so it doesn't really need bread, potatoes or another carbohydrate – if you do add them keep the portion size small.

Beanburgers

The kids are mad about burgers. I think it's as much to do with being able to hold a burger in their hand and munch away to their hearts' content as it is the taste. Meat is an expensive protein and beans are relatively cheap, so by replacing beefburger night with beanburger night you'll save yourself some money and sneak in an alternative protein source.

Cost-wise a beanburger will be about a quarter of the price of a beefburger.

makes 6 burgers

200g cooked chickpeas (see page 21) • 200g cooked kidney beans (see page 21)

1 red pepper, finely chopped • 1 yellow pepper, finely chopped

3 spring onions, finely chopped • 1 teaspoon paprika

1 teaspoon ground cumin • 1 teaspoon ground coriander

2 teaspoons ginger and garlic paste (see page 14)

100g gram (chickpea) flour • sunflower oil for frying

Method

❊ Put the chickpeas and kidney beans in a very large mixing bowl and mash them well using a potato masher. You need to keep some texture but you will want to release some of their natural juices.

❊ Heat a non-stick frying pan on a medium heat.

❊ Add the peppers, spring onions, spices, ginger and garlic paste and half the gram flour to the beans. Get your hands in and mix it all together. Add a little extra gram flour if it seems too wet. Put the remaining flour onto a flat plate.

❊ Shape the mixture into six burgers, then pat them onto the flour on the plate to coat them.

❊ Fry until golden brown and crispy on each side and serve in a bun with your favourite toppings and relish.

Three Bean Chilli

Packed full of an alternative protein source to meat, this bean chilli disguises a number of vegetables in the sauce. It has very little chilli kick, more of an aromatic Mexican flavour, thanks to the addition of spices from your store cupboard. The secret in this great sauce is the slow cooking.

Because you need to start preparation the night before, this recipe is one that I batch cook so I've included enough ingredients for twelve people. Once cool, you can decant the sauce into individual or larger containers to freeze and enjoy another day. It requires organisation but not a huge amount of time to make as you'll find yourself doing a component that takes 10 minutes and then leaving it for a while before stirring.

serves 12

100g dried chickpeas • 100g dried kidney beans • 100g dried flageolet beans

2 tablespoons sunflower oil • 2 onions, chopped • 1 teaspoon ground cumin

1 teaspoon ground coriander • 2 cloves of garlic, finely chopped

1 teaspoon chilli powder • 4 carrots, peeled • 2 tablespoons tomato purée

2 x 400g tins of tomatoes or 800g fresh tomatoes, chopped • 500ml water

Method

❋ The night before cooking this recipe soak and prepare the beans and chickpeas as described on page 21.

❋ At least 3 hours before you want to eat, heat the sunflower oil in a large saucepan on a medium heat. Fry the onions, cumin and coriander until the onions begin to soften.

❋ Add the garlic and chilli powder and continue frying until the garlic is softened as well.

❋ Grate in the carrots and add the tomato purée, stir well until the carrot has heated through.

❋ Pour in the chopped tomatoes. Add the water, stir and bring to a simmer.

❋ Cover the saucepan and simmer for at least 90 minutes, stirring every now and again.

❋ Once cooked, either pulse with a stick blender or mash with a potato masher to get rid of any large lumps of tomato which might not be pleasant for small children.

❋ Strain the soaked beans and pour them directly into the tomato sauce. Bring back to a simmer and cook for a further hour.

❋ Serve with rice and eat with a spoon.

Home-made Baked Beans

Another 'make-ahead' bean dish. You may be wondering why these are called baked beans when there is no baking involved. Well originally they would have been baked in a tin can over an open fire. Nowadays we cook them on the stove, but the name remains the same. We do love them in our house!

serves 8 so makes 2 family meals

200g dried cannellini beans • 1 medium white onion • 2 cloves of garlic
2 medium carrots • 1 tablespoon sunflower oil • 1 tablespoon tomato purée
400g tin of peeled plum tomatoes (whole) in tomato juice
1 tablespoon Worcester sauce

Method

❀ Soak the dried beans in 500ml of water the night before you intend to make this recipe. Make sure they are well covered with water.

❀ Peel and roughly chop the onions, garlic and carrots.

❀ Heat the sunflower oil in a large saucepan (with a lid) on a low heat, then add the onions and garlic. Stir until coated with the oil and then cook for 10 minutes, stirring every now and again. Make sure the saucepan doesn't get too hot, reducing the heat if it looks like the vegetables are beginning to brown.

❀ Add the tomato purée and carrots. Stir until all the vegetables are well coated.

❀ Strain the beans, then pour them, the tinned tomatoes, a litre of hot water and the Worcester sauce into the saucepan. Bring to a simmer. Reduce the heat to very low, cover the saucepan and cook on low for 2 hours.

❀ If not eating immediately, place into sterilised jars and leave to cool before covering. The baked beans will keep for up to 3 weeks in the fridge.

Pilaf with Baked Eggs

A pilaf is a baked rice dish that uses spices to flavour the rice. A kedgeree uses the same spices but isn't baked. This works particularly well as a late supper with a green salad. Do try it out for its delicious simplicity.

serves 4

20g butter • 1 tablespoon sunflower oil • 1 onion, peeled and chopped

1 teaspoon turmeric • 1 teaspoon paprika • 1 teaspoon cumin seeds

1 teaspoon nigella (black onion) seeds • 100g basmati rice

4 eggs

Method

- Preheat a fan oven to 170°C. Put the kettle on to boil.

- Melt the butter and sunflower oil in a saucepan, then add the onion and cook until translucent.

- Pour in the spices and toast in the warm oil until the scents are released. Add the rice and coat in the fragrant oil.

- Transfer the entire contents of the saucepan to an ovenproof dish. Pour in 250ml of hot water and cover the dish with tinfoil. Bake in the oven for 20 minutes.

- Remove the dish from the oven and using the back of a spoon make four wells in the rice. Crack an egg into each well and return the dish (uncovered) to the oven for a further 7 minutes or until the eggs are just cooked.

- Use the runny eggs as a sauce with the rice.

Green Quiche

Kids love to eat food in their hands and if I can hide some 'green stuff' in this great quiche then it's another way to sneak it into their diet. The addition of yoghurt to the quiche mixture, even though it's unsweetened, gives a slight sweetness to the finished dish that the kids love.

serves 6 for lunch or 4 for a main meal

270g roll puff pastry • 50g chard or spinach leaf
50g beetroot tops or finely shredded green cabbage leaves
6 spring onions • 50ml natural yoghurt • 2 medium eggs

Method

❀ Preheat your fan oven to 180°C.

❀ Line an 18cm sandwich tin with greaseproof paper or just grease the tin and dust with flour.

❀ Unroll the puff pastry and cut it to fit the tin.

❀ Wash and chop the chard or spinach and the beetroot tops or cabbage leaves roughly – not too small. Slice the spring onions lengthways.

❀ In a large jug mix the yoghurt and eggs together with a fork before adding the leaves – leave the spring onions out for now. Stir until the egg mixture coats each leaf, then pour into the pastry-lined tin.

❀ Pop the spring onions into the quiche mixture on top of the filling mixture and arrange them in a pattern if you like.

❀ Bake in the oven for 45 minutes and allow to cool a little before serving.

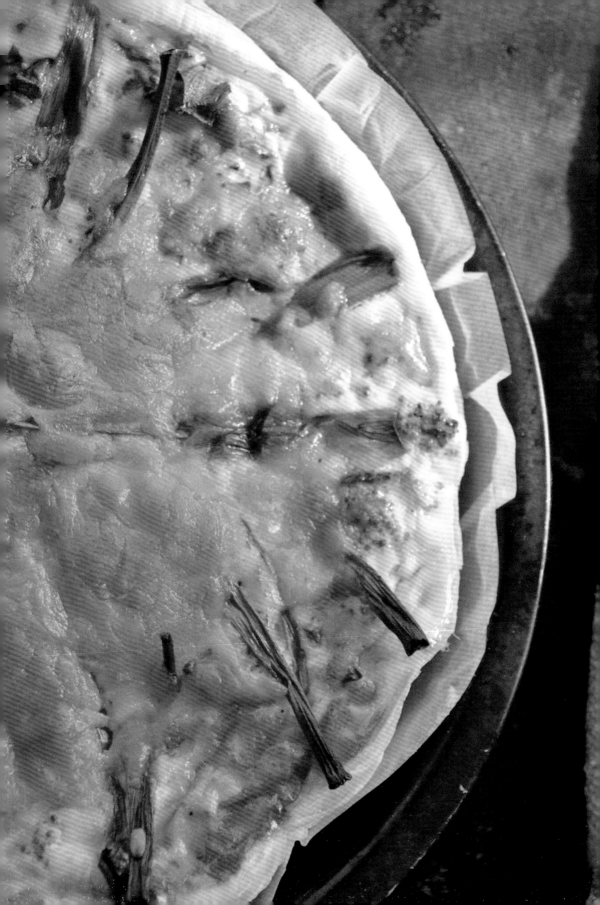

Quiche Cups

There are days when the kids get tired of the everyday humdrum school lunches and they love bringing a cup of quiche in their lunchbox. The key to the success of this quiche is to allow the kids to fill them up themselves before they are baked. They each have a preferred filling – for example, my four-year-old loves cheese and salami, but my toddler loves sweetcorn and peppers. Just work with whatever your kids like the most!

makes 12

50g butter, melted • 1 packet of chilled filo pastry • 4 eggs
3 tablespoons natural yoghurt • 1 red/yellow pepper, chopped
2 spring onions, chopped

Method

❀ Preheat a fan oven to 170°C. Brush a twelve-hole cupcake tin/muffin tray liberally with melted butter and dust lightly with flour.

❀ Cut the filo pastry into squares that are twice the size of the holes in the tin and layer at least three squares into each cup, alternating the angles and brushing the pastry with melted butter in between each layer.

❀ Take a large jug and combine the eggs and yoghurt. Pour the mixture into each individual cup. Fill up to three-quarter level, then sprinkle each cup with the chopped vegetables.

❀ Bake in the oven for 25 minutes. Allow to cool in the tin before tipping out and serving.

Hash Browns

The mixture of potato and onion becomes sweet when you shred them finely. The starch in the potato turns sweet and sticky when it soaks up the onion juices. I love hash browns on their own, hot straight from the pan, but the best way, I think, to contrast the crunchy sweet patties is with scrambled eggs.

makes 12 hash browns which should serve 4 people

2 large potatoes, peeled • 1 medium onion, peeled • 50g plain flour
sunflower oil for sautéing • scrambled eggs to serve

Method

❊ Coarsely grate the potato and onion into a large bowl. Wrap them in a clean tea towel and squeeze out any excess liquid.

❊ Stir in the flour and some salt and pepper and mix well.

❊ Heat the sunflower oil in a large frying pan on a medium heat. Take a tablespoon full of the potato mixture and compact together in your hand before placing in the pan to cook. Turn carefully with a spatula when golden brown on the underside. Once cooked, sit the hash brown on some kitchen paper to drain.

❊ Once all the hash brown mixture is cooked, make your scrambled eggs and serve.

Spanish Breakfast Home Fries

The idea of eating potatoes for breakfast isn't a new one and honestly I can't figure out why we don't do this more in Ireland. Potatoes are a low-fat ingredient and if you have cold spuds left over from the night before this is a great lazy brunch dish as you don't need to stand over a hot stove to make it!

serves 4 for brunch or 2 as a substantial main meal

200g chorizo

500g cooked potatoes

50g frozen peas

Method

❁ Preheat a fan oven to 200°C.

❁ Chop the chorizo into bite-sized chunks and place in a large baking dish. Place in the oven for 15 minutes until the meat is roasted and the oils have been released.

❁ Chop the potatoes into similar-sized chunks.

❁ Remove the dish from the oven. Carefully spoon in the potatoes and toss them around in the amber oil, making sure they are fully coated with the juices.

❁ Return the baking dish to the oven and bake for a further 15 minutes.

❁ Remove from the oven, stir in the frozen peas, cover and allow to rest for 5 minutes before serving.

Chard Potatoes

When new potatoes are in season they're good value and the baby potatoes in particular are so fresh, I like to buy them in bulk. Steaming potatoes is a quick and easy way to cook them with minimal mess. Steam twice as many as you need for a meal because this recipe for cold leftover spuds is a real treat.

serves 4

1 tablespoon sunflower oil • 1 onion, peeled and thinly sliced
1 tablespoon harissa powder (or a pinch each of paprika, ground cumin, dried
coriander and oregano) • 500g cooked potatoes, chopped into chunks
10 leaves of fresh chard, stalks removed and finely chopped, leaves roughly torn
poached eggs to serve (optional)

Method

- Bring a large frying pan to a medium heat and pour in the oil. Add the onions and fry until soft and golden.

- Add the harissa powder to the pan and stir around to release the aroma into the oil.

- Toss the cooked potatoes in the oil and move gently every couple of minutes so that they get a red hue. After 10 minutes stir in the chard leaves and stalks. These will cook in about 3 minutes.

- Serve immediately and top with a poached egg if you like.

Potato Salad

For picnic lunches or lazy suppers, potato salad ticks all the boxes for using up leftover boiled or steamed potatoes. The potato takes care of the carbohydrate in your meal, so you can dress it up with boiled eggs, plenty of green leaves, slices of tomato, cucumber, beetroot, onions or whatever you like.

serves 4

4–6 steamed/boiled potatoes, cooled • 100ml crème fraiche
4 large chive leaves • 1 handful of parsley, finely chopped

Method

❁ Using a sharp knife, cut the potatoes into bite-sized chunks and put into a large bowl.

❁ Pour in the crème fraiche.

❁ Using sharp scissors cut the chives into small pieces and let them fall into the bowl. Tumble in the parsley.

❁ Stir well until every piece of potato is coated.

❁ Crack some black pepper on top and season with salt to taste.

❁ Serve with a sprinkling of pink chive flowers if they are in season.

Sausage Casserole

When sausage meat is on special I buy up a couple of packets of it. I freeze the meat and use it through the year to make sausage rolls and this sausage casserole.

serves 5

150g sausage meat • 1 onion • 7 medium potatoes
2 carrots, peeled • 350ml hot water • ½ small green or white cabbage
200g frozen peas • 1 apple or a handful of raisins (optional)

Method

❀ Roll the sausage meat into ping-pong sized balls. Heat a large saucepan on high and fry off the meatballs until they become brown. There's no need to use oil to cook here as the sausage meat is fatty enough. Remove them from the saucepan once brown and drain on some kitchen paper.

❀ There should be enough fat left in the saucepan to cook the vegetables. Peel and finely chop the onion and sizzle in the oil for 5 minutes.

❀ Peel and chop the potatoes and carrots into bite-sized chunks. Add the potatoes to the saucepan and allow them to become coated in the sausage fat. Fry them for a few minutes before adding the carrots and then the hot water. Cover and simmer the mixture for 20 minutes.

❀ Finely shred the cabbage and stir into the casserole.

❀ Pour in the frozen peas and the apple, roughly chopped, or raisins if using. Once the peas have thawed, the potatoes should be cooked (use a fork to check).

❀ Serve immediately.

Hearty Meals

I believe that even if you need to eat frugally, you should not have to feel like you're compromising on flavour, taste or quality. Our main meal is a key part of my philosophy of great food on a budget. These recipes for hearty meals aren't just delicious, but will fill you up well and also contain plenty of nutrients, vitamins, iron and fibre, all essential for good health.

Whole Sea Bass in a Parcel

I don't know what it is, but people don't seem to buy whole fish on the bone. Yet this is the cheapest way to pick up nutritious fish at the fishmonger. Is it because you don't like an eye looking up at you on the plate? Buy the whole fish and ask for the head to be removed. It's no extra cost and they will have no problem doing it for you!

I like to cook whole fish on the barbecue, but this recipe works just as well in the oven, although it does need a longer cooking time.

You will need to assemble a parcel to cook each fish in before you get all your ingredients together. Cut 30cm square pieces of baking parchment and tinfoil. Put the baking parchment on top of the tinfoil and fold them in half. Fold 1cm of the short sides over twice to seal the ends, so that you only have one open side.

serves 2 ♥

2 tablespoons sesame oil • 1 whole sea bass (head removed if you prefer)

2 spring onions, shredded • 1 carrot, peeled and finely shredded

1 piece of ginger about the size of your thumb, peeled and finely shredded

2 cloves of garlic, finely sliced • 1 red chilli, finely sliced • soy sauce

Method

❀ Assemble a parcel as described above. Splash the sesame oil into the parcel.

❀ Take the fish and stuff the cavity with the shredded and sliced ingredients. If they don't all fit, toss any extra into the parcel. Splash a little soy sauce over the whole fish and tip it into the parcel, making sure that you have enough space around the edge to seal the parcel.

❀ Seal the remaining open end by folding over twice.

❀ Bake on the barbecue for 12 minutes or in the oven at 210°C for 25 minutes. Serve in the parcel with crusty bread to dunk in the juices.

Pea Risotto

It's a little family secret that we use pudding rice to make our risotto. Okay, so it's not classic Italian cooking, but it is cheaper than buying Arborio rice! Pick up pudding rice in the dessert section of the supermarket near the tinned fruits. The high starch content is perfect for this recipe and you will end up with luscious creamy risotto that tastes like the real deal. I also use cheddar instead of parmesan to keep costs down – if you prefer the original Italian cheese and can afford it, exchange the cheddar for parmesan. I promise I won't tell anyone if you don't!

serves 4

20g butter • 150g pudding rice
400ml warm vegetable stock or chicken stock (see page 107) • 1 cup frozen peas
2 kabanossi sausages, chopped (these are optional and you will find them in the
Polish food section) • 50g cheddar cheese, chopped into small pieces
4 chives, finely chopped • some chive flowers to decorate

Method

❁ Melt the butter in a large saucepan on a medium heat. Toss the rice in the butter for about 5 minutes until you hear a sizzling sound and you're sure that the rice is coated.

❁ Using a ladle, add a little of the warm vegetable stock to the rice. Stir well until it is absorbed. Repeat when you can't see the liquid anymore. Keep on repeating until your stockpot is empty.

❁ Stir in the frozen peas, then after 3 or 4 minutes, the sausages and cheese. Cook for a further 2 minutes until the sausages are warmed through.

❁ Just before serving stir in the chopped chives. When serving, decorate with chive flowers.

❁ Eat with a spoon!

Herb Prawns

As a rule I like to introduce fresh herbs to food after the main cooking has been done. Herbs burn and don't taste at their best unless they are freshly torn or chopped on top of your food. However, a herb oil can impart a lot of the flavour while cooking, with none of the burnt element. Herb oil is easily made by popping a sprig each of rosemary, thyme and parsley into a small bottle or jar containing 150ml sunflower oil. You then shake it well every day for a week. The oil will keep for about a month and it is so fragrant you'll get plenty of use from it.

This recipe works just as well with small prawns as with the larger gambas pictured here. You just need to reduce the cooking time. Because I cook them on the barbecue, I leave the shells on. Everybody digs in together at the table and shells them. It's a real talking point at any party and the oil adds just a little bit of extra flavour.

Prawns can be expensive to buy so there are a couple of options to keep costs down. The first is to buy frozen prawns if you're on a serious budget. You will need to defrost them before cooking on the barbecue. Prawns are always cheaper to buy quayside, so if you live close to a harbour then a trip every now and again to stock up the freezer will save you plenty of money. The less processing that a prawn has gone through, the cheaper it will be, so buy with the head and feet on, and raw where possible.

serves 4

500g fresh prawns or gambas • 30ml herb oil (see left) • fresh lemon juice

Method

❉ Pour the prawns into a large sandwich bag, add the herb oil on top, followed by a sprinkling of sea salt. Seal and shake gently.

❉ Cook the prawns directly on the barbecue grill or a hot griddle pan. Turn after 4 minutes and cook for a further 4 minutes. Serve immediately with a squeeze of fresh lemon juice.

Lamb Burger with Cucumber Pickle

When lamb mince is good value I tend to stock up. Lamb burgers offer a lovely alternative to a regular beefburger. However, lamb mince can be very fatty, so check your labelling to make sure that you get mince with a lower fat content. About 10% is fine but always grill or griddle lamb mince rather than fry. Strain the juices off the pan regularly into a ceramic mug and leave to cool before discarding into the bin.

serves 4 ♥

for the burgers

200g minced lamb • ½ white onion, peeled and finely chopped
1 sprig of mint, finely chopped

for cucumber pickle

½ cucumber • 1 sprig of mint, finely chopped • 1 chilli, finely sliced
1 tablespoon cider vinegar

Method

❀ To make the pickle, cut the cucumber in half lengthways and scoop out the seeds. Slice finely then combine with the other pickle ingredients about 30 minutes before serving.

❀ For the burgers, combine the lamb, onion and mint in a large bowl. Shape into four decent-sized burgers. Cook on a dry frying pan, or ideally a griddle pan or barbecue, on a medium heat. Turn after 10 minutes and cook for a further 10 minutes. Press down on the meat a little with a spatula to ensure that you get more cooking surface area.

❀ Serve with the cucumber pickle, a baked potato and green salad.

'Mac' and Cheese

I don't use macaroni in this recipe as the pasta shape can be hard to find in Irish supermarkets and when you do find it, it'll be more expensive than cheaper shapes! I use fusilli pasta (known as spirals in our house) and they suck in the sauce just as well.

When you've kids in the house the value of having a freshly cooked dinner in a rapid space of time shouldn't be underestimated. If you can afford to pick up six silicone cupcake cases they are a great addition to your storage abilities. It's best not to use paper cases as they will stick to the macaroni in the chilling process. Alternatively a silicone muffin tray will work just as well. If necessary you can just cook the mixture in a baking dish, and divide into portions once it's cooked.

serves 6 small children

100g dried fusilli pasta • 200ml milk • 100g grated cheddar cheese
50g frozen sweetcorn • 50g frozen peas

Method

❊ Preheat a fan oven to 180°C. Line a cupcake tin/muffin tray with 6 silicone cupcake cases.

❊ Boil the pasta in water for 2 minutes less than the recommended cooking time so that it is not entirely cooked. Drain and set to one side.

❊ Heat the milk slowly in a large saucepan. When it is almost at boiling point, sprinkle in three-quarters of the grated cheese bit by bit. Stir well until it is melted into the milk. I find a small hand whisk is easier than a wooden spoon at this stage.

❊ Add the pasta to the milk sauce, followed by the sweetcorn and peas. Stir until everything is well coated.

❊ Divide the pasta and sauce equally between the six cupcake cases. Sprinkle over the remaining cheese. Bake in the oven for 15 minutes.

❊ Serve immediately or leave to cool to room temperature before freezing the whole cases overnight. The following day slide the silicone cases off the 'cupcakes' and wash for reuse. Put the cupcakes into a freezer bag and they will keep for up to a month in the freezer.

❊ To reheat, simply microwave until heated through.

Meatballs with Crispy Potatoes

For a quick and tasty dinner using up some leftover potatoes, this is a nice quick option.

serves 2 adults and 2 children

200g minced meat (beef or lamb) • 2 tablespoons tomato purée
6 cold cooked potatoes • 2 tablespoons sunflower oil

Method

❀ Preheat a fan oven to 180°C.

❀ Mix the minced meat, tomato purée and some salt and pepper together in a large bowl. Wet your hands and roll ping-pong-ball-sized meatballs.

❀ Roughly chop the potatoes, or bash them with a fork, and then drizzle with the sunflower oil. Place them in a heatproof baking dish and add the meatballs.

❀ Bake in the oven for 45 minutes.

❀ Serve with a light salad or chunky cut vegetables which are convenient for little hands.

Boozy Mussels

It's always better to buy mussels from your fishmonger or supermarket as most of us don't have the facilities at home to clean them. I don't mean scrubbing the bearded bits off the outside, I mean the sand inside the mussels. They do need a good clean before cooking and so your fishmonger will put them in a cleaning tank before he sells them. No matter how juicy or big they look on the shore, I'd recommend you don't collect or cook your own mussels unless you're an expert!

In hot weather I prefer to cook fish on the barbecue because it's so quick and I am not a fan of slaving over the grill in the sunshine. Mussels are one of the cheapest options in the fish aisle but, as with prawns, the more processing the more expensive they will be. So always buy plain mussels in their shells to keep costs down.

serves 4

600g fresh mussels, cleaned • 2 chillies, finely sliced
2cm piece of ginger, finely sliced • a good glug of beer

Method

❀ Take a piece of tinfoil big enough to hold all the mussels and put it shiny side upwards on a smooth surface. Cut a piece of greaseproof paper the same size and put it on top. Fold them in half, and then double fold the two opposite open edges so that you get an envelope.

❀ Make sure all the mussels are tightly closed or will close when given a firm tap on your work surface. Discard any that do not or that have broken shells.

❀ Pour all the ingredients into the envelope and seal the open end with a double fold. Shake it a little, not too much, to make sure everything is coated.

❀ Bake on the barbecue for 15 minutes on a top rack or for 7 minutes on a hot rack near piping hot coals. Alternatively, cook in a hot oven at 220°C for 15 minutes. All the mussels should be open. If you find one or two that are still closed, discard them before serving.

❀ I normally open and pour the contents onto one big plate and serve in the middle of the table with lots of crusty bread to mop up the juices.

Pulled Pork

I've called this recipe 'pulled pork', but really that's just using a term that has recently come from the far side of the Atlantic for something we've been cooking for years. Pulled pork is a piece of pork, cooked slowly and rubbed with spices, that's so soft you can pull it apart with a spoon. Often you would drizzle it with, or dunk it in, a sauce.

You can slow cook any cut of meat, but a high fat content does help with the flavour. This recipe works for chops in a slow cooker if you have one, but I've given instructions for the oven.

serves 4

3 pork chops, preferably still on the bone and with fat still on

200ml vegetable stock • 2 tomatoes, chopped

1 eating apple, chopped • 3 cloves of garlic, chopped

1 teaspoon chilli powder • 1 tablespoon cider vinegar

Method

🌸 Preheat a fan oven to 140°C.

🌸 Take a large ovenproof dish and combine all the ingredients, except the pork, with some salt and pepper, mashing down a bit with a fork where you can. Slide the pork chops into the mixture and cover the dish tightly with tinfoil. Put the dish on a baking tray for ease of removal from the oven.

🌸 Bake for 4 hours. Remove from the oven and mash the ingredients together with a fork, pulling out any bones.

🌸 Serve with fresh lettuce leaves, chopped green pepper and noodles.

Ragu

The old family favourite, spaghetti bolognaise, is normally made with minced beef, but I make mine with stewing beef and send it off for a long, slow cook before serving. This is a great recipe to scale up and have on standby in the freezer.

serves 4

1 tablespoon sunflower oil • 1 onion, peeled and diced
2 cloves of garlic, peeled and diced • 2 carrots, peeled and roughly chopped
2 peppers, peeled and roughly chopped • 300g stewing beef
2 tablespoons tomato purée • dash of vinegar
fresh herbs – basil, parsley, oregano (optional)

Method

* Heat the sunflower oil in a large saucepan over a medium heat. Add the onion and garlic and fry until translucent.

* Add the carrots and peppers, fry for 3 minutes.

* Add the beef one tablespoonful at a time and fry a little in the oil until it turns brown, before moving to the side of the pan and adding the next tablespoon of meat.

* When all the meat is browned stir through the tomato purée, then pour over 200ml of hot water, season with a pinch of salt, pepper and sugar and add the vinegar.

* Cover the saucepan, reduce the heat to low and leave to simmer for at least three-quarters of an hour or up to 2 hours – the longer the better. Stir every now and again to ensure that nothing is sticking to the bottom of the saucepan. Add a small amount of water if the mixture seems too dry.

* Fold in chopped fresh herbs if using before serving with your favourite pasta shape.

Twice-Cooked Pork Ribs

A sticky treat, it's worth the time it takes to make these ribs – they're not labour intensive, they just need long, slow cooking.

serves 4

for the ribs

1 rack of pork ribs, separated (get your butcher to do this) • 1 onion, peeled
2 sticks of celery • 1 carrot, peeled

for the rub

50g dark brown muscovado sugar • 50ml apple juice
1 teaspoon ground ginger • 1 teaspoon paprika

Method

❀ Preheat a fan oven to 150°C.

❀ First get the ribs under way: roughly chop the vegetables into large chunks and put in a deep baking tray (I use my grill tray with the rack removed). Rest the ribs on top. Pour 200ml of warm water into the tray. Cover the baking tray with tinfoil and seal tightly.

❀ Bake in the oven for 2 hours.

❀ After the ribs have been cooking for 90 minutes, heat the rub ingredients in a small saucepan until bubbling. Set to one side and leave to cool for 20 minutes (although you can use it while hot, you might get scalded!).

❀ Remove the ribs from the oven and carefully peel back the tinfoil. Turn the oven up to 200°C. Take a shallow baking sheet, line it with tinfoil and sit the grill rack on top. Lift the ribs onto the rack and brush with the rub. The vegetables on which the ribs cooked can be discarded.

❀ Roast the ribs in the oven for 20 minutes, then serve with tomato relish (see page 206) and steamed rice or a baked potato and salad.

Mild Spiced Beef Stir-Fry

For last-minute meals, there is nothing as swift as a stir-fry. The kids love the mild spicing in this dish and the adults do too. On cold or wet days I add a little water to the pot which creates a broth that they like to slurp at the end. Stewing beef is one of the cheapest cuts you can get from the butcher apart from mince. If you slice it very finely you will get a beautiful piece of beef without having to stew it for ages.

serves 4

1 tablespoon sunflower oil • 1 onion, finely sliced

1 teaspoon ginger and garlic paste (see page 14)

½ teaspoon ground cumin • ½ teaspoon ground coriander

½ teaspoon cayenne pepper • 200g stewing beef, very finely sliced

2 carrots, peeled and finely sliced • 1 small head of broccoli, chopped into florets

1 yellow pepper, sliced • 2 tablespoons fish sauce • 1 handful of coriander leaves

Method

❀ Heat a very large saucepan or wok on a medium heat. Add the sunflower oil and then the onion. Allow to sizzle for about 3 minutes before adding the paste, cumin, coriander and cayenne pepper. Stir around so that the spices coat the onions.

❀ Add the beef, one quarter at a time, so as to prevent the beef from stewing at the start. Make sure it gets coated in the spices and nicely browned before adding the next batch.

❀ Finally, add in the carrots, broccoli and pepper. Stir well and cover the saucepan for 10 minutes. Remove the lid, pour in the fish sauce and stir again. At this point you can add some water to make a broth if you like, but the water content from the peppers and carrots will give you a little anyway.

❀ Serve with fresh coriander on top and steamed or boiled rice.

Cider Mustard Pork

I used to steer away from lean pork loin because it can be expensive, but when you break it down, a pork loin contains a lot of meat protein and is low in fat. You'll get two family meals from this recipe so make once and freeze half when it has cooled to room temperature.

serves 10

1 pork loin (about 600g) • 50g plain flour • 1 tablespoon sunflower oil
1 onion, finely chopped • 2 cloves of garlic, finely chopped
200ml cider • 3 carrots, peeled and chopped
75g frozen peas • 1 teaspoon wholegrain mustard

Method

❄ Slice the pork thinly. Put the flour, with a pinch of salt and pepper, into a sandwich bag and add the pork into the bag. Shake until it is well coated.

❄ Take a large saucepan and place on a medium heat. Pour in the sunflower oil and fry the pork until golden on each side. It won't be completely cooked through. Remove from the pan and sit on kitchen paper to drain.

❄ Add the onion to the pan and sizzle for 5 minutes before adding the chopped garlic. Return the pork to the frying pan and pour in the cider and carrots. Simmer for 15 minutes before adding the peas. Allow to heat through, then stir in the mustard.

❄ Serve with steamed potatoes or rice.

Fish Scale Pie

Involving the kids in making this tasty dish is the key to making sure they eat it! While they may not relish dealing with the fish and the sauce, there isn't a child in my house who will say no when it comes to rolling and cutting pastry! By layering some simple circles, the pie looks like it has 'fish scales' so it's a feast for the eyes and for the belly.

serves 4 ♡

200ml milk • 1 bay leaf • 2 whole peppercorns • 200g fresh or frozen fish

30g butter • 50g plain flour, plus extra for dusting

75g frozen sweetcorn • 75g frozen peas

200g shortcrust pastry – ready-made or see Jam Tarts recipe (see page 242)

milk to brush the 'scales'

Method

❁ Heat the milk, bay leaf and peppercorns to a gentle simmer. Cook the fish in the milk. If it is in small chunks they should only take 10 minutes, for larger pieces allow 15 minutes. Scoop out the fish and set to one side. Pick out the bay leaf and peppercorns and throw away. Pour the hot milk into a mug.

❁ Melt the butter in the same saucepan, sprinkle in the flour and cook for 5 minutes. Add the milk from the mug, one quarter at a time, and stir each time until it is well mixed and you have a smooth paste. Add a little hot water until you have a thick sauce.

❁ Pour the sweetcorn and peas into the sauce. Turn off the heat. Stir in the fish.

❁ Preheat a fan oven to 180°C.

❁ Grease an 18cm sandwich tin and dust with flour. Dust a flat surface with flour, divide the pastry into two sections and roll out one round to line the bottom and sides of the tin.

❁ Pour the fish sauce into the lined tin and roll out the second section of pastry. Cut out lots of small circles with a glass or a biscuit cutter. Combine and re-roll any trimmings as necessary.

❁ Layer the 'scales' up to coat the top of the pie. Brush with milk and bake for 90 minutes. Serve immediately for a complete meal.

'Only Codding' Fish Cakes

These are light, fluffy fish cakes with a crunchy crumb coating, and a sweet flavour that kids will love. Make life easy on yourself and cook double quantities of the fish you need when you're making the fish scale pie (see page 179). While I call them 'only codding' fish cakes, I rarely make these with cod – in fact the picture you see is made with haddock. Other varieties of fish that work just as well include ling (also known as cod-ling), whiting or pollock, but there is nothing stopping you using an oily fish such as salmon or mackerel either. Cod tends to be the most expensive fish on the shelf, so if you change the fish in the cakes depending on the season or special offer, they will be more economical.

serves 5

200g stale breadcrumbs • 70ml milk • 200g cooked fish
1 red pepper • 3 spring onions • 1 handful of coriander
2 tablespoons sunflower oil

Method

❁ Put half the breadcrumbs into a large bowl and pour over the milk. Allow to soak for about 5 minutes.

❁ Add the cooked fish to the breadcrumbs and mash with a fork.

❁ If you have a mini-blender or stick blender, blend the pepper, onions and coriander into a loose paste, otherwise chop them as finely as you can. Mash this into the fish and breadcrumb mixture.

❁ Heat the sunflower oil in a non-stick frying pan on a medium heat.

❁ Take the remaining half of the dry breadcrumbs and put them on a flat plate. Use your hands to shape the fish mixture into small rounds, then pat into the breadcrumbs on either side to get a crumb coating.

❁ Fry in the hot oil until golden on each side. Serve with relish and a green salad.

Paprika Chicken Wings

Chicken wings are one of the cheapest pieces of meat that you can buy. They can be fun to eat and the key to making them succulent is to cook them twice.

serves 2 adults and 2 children

250g chicken wings

1 onion

4 cloves of garlic

2 teaspoons paprika

1 tablespoon sunflower oil

Method

✿ Preheat a fan oven to 170°C.

✿ Take a large roasting dish. Spread the chicken wings evenly over the dish.

✿ Peel the onion and divide it into quarters and add it to the dish. Peel the garlic and add it too. Sprinkle the contents of the roasting dish with the paprika.

✿ Cover tightly with tinfoil and bake in the oven for 90 minutes.

✿ Remove the wings from the oven. Heat a non-stick frying pan on a high heat, pour in the sunflower oil. Fry the wings in the oil until the skin starts to crisp up and turn brown. Pat dry with kitchen paper before serving with fried rice (see page 97).

Roasted-Vegetable Lasagne

Roasted vegetables on their own can be a hearty main meal, so consider making double the vegetable quantity if you can so that you make enough to eat and then prepare the lasagne later. The addition of nutmeg to the white lasagne sauce lifts the roasted vegetables. I know it's a small amount but it just adds a little extra something to the flavour.

serves 4

1 small turnip • 3 carrots • 1 small cauliflower • 2 tablespoons sunflower oil
1 onion • 2 cloves of garlic • 400g tin of chopped tomatoes • 30g butter
50g plain flour • 200ml milk • ¼ teaspoon grated nutmeg
200g dried lasagne (about 12 sheets)

Method

❁ Preheat a fan oven to 190°C.

❁ Peel the turnip and carrots and chop them, and the cauliflower, into large chunks. Put them in a large roasting dish, then toss the vegetables in 1 tablespoon of the sunflower oil. Roast in the oven for 1 hour.

❁ In the meantime, take a small saucepan and heat the remaining sunflower oil over a medium heat. Chop and sizzle the onions until translucent (this will take about 10 minutes).

❁ Chop the garlic and add to the onions, sizzle for another 5 minutes before pouring the tomatoes on top. Simmer the tomato sauce for 20 minutes.

❁ Melt the butter in a small saucepan, sprinkle over the flour, and allow to cook for 5 minutes before adding the milk bit by bit until you have a thick sauce. Season with salt and pepper, then stir in the grated nutmeg.

❁ Assemble the lasagne in a roasting dish. Put 4 tablespoons of the roasted vegetables in the bottom of the dish, cover with the tomato sauce, then with dried lasagne sheets, before topping the sheets with the creamy white sauce, then vegetables again. Continue to alternate the sauces and use the roasted vegetables. Make sure you reserve some of the white sauce for the final, top layer. Bake in the oven for 60 minutes before serving.

Beetroot and Ricotta Pizza

This is pizza – but not as you know it! The beetroot is both savoury and sweet at the same time, the ricotta is deliciously smooth and a little drizzle of honey on top brings it all together. The toppings are not added until the dough is cooked. You can eat this pizza hot or cold. I prefer mine hot with the cold topping contrasting.

serves 5

for the pizza base

250g strong white flour • 1 tablespoon olive oil • 1 teaspoon dried yeast
½ teaspoon salt

for the topping

2 cooked beetroot • 3 tablespoons olive oil • 100g ricotta
honey to taste

Method

❀ Mix the flour and olive oil together until you get a crumbly texture. Stir in the dried yeast and salt, then add 150ml of cold water gradually until you have a soft dough. You may not need all the water.

❀ Knead for 15–20 minutes. Cover and leave to rise for about 3 hours.

❀ Preheat a fan oven to 220°C. Line a baking tray with greaseproof paper, then sprinkle with flour or semolina.

❀ Divide the dough into 5 pieces, roll as thinly as possible and bake, one at a time, on the prepared tray until they are all golden brown. Allow to cool a little on a rack.

❀ Blend together the cooked beetroot, olive oil and some salt and pepper until you get a smooth paste. Spread on the warm pizza base, top with a large spoon of ricotta and a drizzle of honey.

Turkey Dumpling Broth

Breast of turkey is often very reasonably priced, but it can be tricky to know what to do with it. Even the mince can have a bit of a bland flavour. This dumpling broth is fat free and tasty and doesn't take long to make or cook. The kids love fishing out their dumplings and eating them with cocktail sticks before slurping the broth!

serves 5

75ml milk • 100g breadcrumbs • 1 mild chilli
2 handfuls of coriander stalks and leaves • 5 spring onions
2 teaspoons ginger and garlic paste (see page 14)
200g turkey mince • splash of soy sauce
2 carrots, peeled and sliced
1 red pepper, sliced

Method

❋ Pour the milk over the breadcrumbs and leave to soak.

❋ Cut the chilli in half. Put one half into a jug with half the coriander, half the spring onions and half the ginger and garlic paste. Mince using a stick blender, if you have one, otherwise just chop them all very finely.

❋ Pour this mixture on top of the breadcrumbs. Add the turkey mince and mix everything together using your hands (I use plastic/rubber gloves for this to stop the garlic, chilli and ginger from getting onto my hands).

❋ Pour 500ml of hot water (or chicken stock, see page 107) into a large saucepan and put onto a medium heat until it is simmering. Stir in the remaining ginger and garlic paste along with a splash of soy sauce, the carrots and the red pepper.

❋ Use your hands to shape ping-pong sized balls of the turkey dumplings and drop them into the simmering broth. Simmer for 12 minutes. Serve the broth and dumplings with the remaining spring onions and fresh coriander on top. The remaining chilli can be sliced and added to the broth if you like a bit of extra heat or left out if you don't want the broth to be too spicy.

Paprika Beef with Bacon

Take the cheapest cut of beef you can buy at the butchers. This meal is meant to be slow braised. Don't worry about gristle, it will all fall away after cooking for such a long period of time.

serves 5

5 rashers of smoked streaky bacon
200g stewing beef in one large piece, not in chunks
1 tablespoon sunflower oil • 3 teaspoons paprika
400g tin of chopped tomatoes

Method

❁ Cut the rashers of bacon in half and cut the beef into 10 pieces. Wrap each half rasher around a piece of beef and secure with a cocktail stick.

❁ Heat the sunflower oil on medium in a large, heavy-bottomed saucepan or a crockpot. Sprinkle the paprika over the sunflower oil and allow it to cook in the oil for 3 minutes.

❁ Add the bacon-wrapped beef pieces, one by one, and brown in the paprika oil. Turn the heat to low once all the beef has browned.

❁ Pour the tomatoes on top. Stir well. Cover and simmer on low for at least 4 hours. Top up the liquid with water from the kettle if you notice the level getting low.

❁ Serve with crusty bread or rice.

Simple Sides and Nibbles

If, like me, you choose to cook roast meat some days, then having some simple sides to hand is essential. Many of these also make brilliant sandwich fillings or additions to a lunchbox as well as side dishes for a main meal. The key is that they are simple?

Coleslaw

I got this coleslaw recipe from my mother who has been making a variation on this recipe for years. Whenever there's a family barbecue it's a given that she will bring this coleslaw along and there is rarely any left over to take home for sandwiches the next day!

The key to preparing this simple coleslaw is to prepare the individual components up to three days beforehand. You can then combine them at the last minute. So if you're planning a barbecue on Sunday, get this out of the way on Friday evening and then leave the ingredients to one side. If you need to make enough for a large party just stick to the ratio of carrot to cabbage and always mix just before serving, as the carrot tends to bleed into the mixture. If you like to add herbs or a slight onion flavour, then chop some chives and parsley into the mixture.

serves 8

1 large carrot • 1 quarter head of white cabbage

2 tablespoons good quality mayonnaise (reduced fat if you're watching calories)

2 tablespoons natural yoghurt (low fat/fat free if you're on a diet)

1 tablespoon cider vinegar • cracked black pepper

Method

❀ Peel and grate the carrot. If preparing for mixing at a later stage, then place the grated carrot into a plastic, sealable freezer bag, seal and put it into the bottom crisper drawer of your fridge.

❀ Using a good sharp knife, remove the core from the cabbage, peel off the outer, softer leaves (probably about 3) and discard these. Cut the cabbage finely into thin lengths. Repeat the step above with the freezer bag if preparing for another day.

❀ To serve, take the large bowl and measure the remaining ingredients into the bottom of the bowl and stir until they create a thin dressing. Add the cabbage and carrot and mix well until loosely coated with the dressing.

Author's Note: White cabbage is very good for you and is a tasty snack all on its own. I use it a lot as a simple snack before dinner and we typically eat it raw, finely chopped with a squeeze of lemon and a sprinkling of sea salt and cracked black pepper over the top. Think of it as a fat free, high-fibre alternative to the chips and dips that normally grace a party table. For some added protein (and, I'm afraid, fat content), consider sprinkling the cabbage with cashew nuts if you can get them for a good price.

Caramelised Onions

When I get one amazing ingredient I want to make the most of it! We can grow fantastic onions in Ireland. They are so easy to sow and grow: all they need is a little bit of sun and some sandy soil and you can have buckets of onions on the table every autumn.

The beauty of using onions in this way is that you don't have to do much hard work to get the most amazing flavours. Caramelised onions are beautiful with red meat, stirred into a sauce or mashed onto toast with a little grilled cheese on top. The jar, once cold, will keep in the fridge for up to five days.

fills a 300ml jar

1 tablespoon sunflower oil • 1 tablespoon butter • 5 medium brown onions

1 teaspoon sea salt • 1 teaspoon sugar or honey

½ teaspoon fresh cracked black pepper

Method

❀ Heat the oil and butter in a large, wide-bottomed saucepan on a low heat.

❀ Slice the onions as thinly as possible. Don't stress too much if your pieces aren't perfect. The reason why I say to chop them thinly is to increase the surface area for caramelisation.

❀ Pour the onions, salt, sugar or honey and black pepper into the saucepan. Stir regularly for the first 15 minutes until the onions start to soften.

❀ Cook for a further hour stirring every 10 minutes to turn over the onions. You should have golden-brown sticky onions. If they're not quite there, continue for a further 10 minutes, but at this point watch out for burning at the bottom of the saucepan.

Tomato Confit

You can pick up overripe tomatoes for a song in most grocers and supermarkets. People don't seem to like squishy tomatoes – which is great news if you want to get loads of anti-oxidants and not have to pay a fortune for them either!

To confit is to cook an item by submerging it in oil. This is a cheat's version though, as I can't leave a pot of oil simmering on the hob with kids in the house.

fills a 300ml jar

5 cloves of garlic (I know it sounds like a lot but they get sweeter as they confit)
150g fresh tomatoes, sliced
150ml olive oil (plain, cheap olive oil – not virgin or extra virgin)

Method

❋ Preheat a fan oven to 150°C.

❋ Take a loaf tin, pour in the olive oil and then submerge the tomatoes and garlic in the oil. Season with some salt and pepper.

❋ Bake in the oven for 2 hours. Remove and allow to cool before decanting into sterilised glass jars and sealing.

❋ The confit tomatoes will keep for up to 1 month in the fridge. One tablespoon-full per person stirred into warm pasta makes a perfect sauce topped with a little cheese. A splash of balsamic vinegar added to some of the oil and tomato also makes a delicious salad dressing.

Crispy Corn Kernels

These came about as a result of me yearning for holiday food! It has been years since I've had a holiday to sunny climes. I find the best way to remember a place is to recreate the food I love to eat there.

When you buy these crispy corn kernels on the European mainland they are huge, far bigger than the size you can get here. I have to make do with the standard popping corn that you can buy in the supermarket and it makes an exact flavour replica, if a little smaller in the mouth.

makes plenty for 4 to share

100g popping corn • 20ml sunflower oil

Method

* You will need to soak the kernels before you do anything. Put the corn in a large resealable jar. Cover it with water. Leave in a warm spot in the kitchen and shake twice a day for four days. At the end of the fourth day, strain off the liquid.

* Put the corn in a saucepan and add 200ml of fresh water. Simmer for 90 minutes. Drain off the liquid and pat the corn dry.

* Put the sunflower oil in the bottom of a saucepan. Pour in the corn kernels. Bring the oil to a low heat and sizzle the kernels for 15 minutes. Drain on kitchen paper and dredge with salt.

* Eat with tart lemonade, preferably in the sunshine!

Garlic Roll-Up

This is an alternative to garlic bread and is great with any meal. It is very easy to make and can be served at a family get-together where you can smugly take all the compliments for a stunning-looking dish!

serves 6

50g butter, softened • 1 clove of garlic, finely chopped
1 handful of fresh chopped oregano and thyme
270g roll of chilled, ready-made puff pastry

Method

❋ Preheat a fan oven to 180°C. Line an 18cm sandwich tin with non-stick grease-proof paper.

❋ Mash together the butter, garlic and herbs, and season to taste.

❋ Unroll the puff pastry and spread the butter mixture over the pastry. Roll the pastry up tight like a Swiss roll. Cut into 2½cm thick pieces. Stand each piece on its side in the sandwich tin to build up the roll-up – they will be barely touching but will expand into each other in the baking process.

❋ Bake in the oven for 25 minutes, until golden brown on top. Allow it to cool a little on a wire rack before serving.

Cauliflower with Harissa and Chilli

This is about as different from cauliflower cheese as you're going to get! When I was younger I spent some time in the Middle East and it has really shaped my food tastes. I love the spicy flavours permeating the cauliflower, which carries the chilli and seasonings so well. It also has a fabulous orange colour! Harissa is normally sold as a paste or a powder, but if you cannot find it you can make it yourself by combining the spice ingredients below.

serves 4

1 tablespoon sunflower oil • ½ teaspoon coriander • ½ teaspoon cayenne pepper
½ teaspoon cumin • ½ teaspoon dried garlic • ½ cauliflower, chopped into florets
1 fresh chilli, sliced

Method

※ Heat the sunflower oil in a large, wide-bottomed saucepan on a medium heat. Once warm, add the dry spices and garlic and stir around until their aroma fills the air. Pour in the chopped cauliflower and stir well to make sure it is coated in the oil.

※ Add 100ml of hot water, stir again and cover the saucepan for 5 minutes.

※ Remove the lid, strain the cauliflower from the water and put in a large serving bowl. Sprinkle with freshly sliced chilli.

※ This dish is also lovely the following day as a cold salad dish providing the cauliflower hasn't been overcooked. The trick here is to cut the vegetable into large, chunky pieces.

Piri Piri Broccoli with Lemon

Broccoli is one of those superfoods that I think needs very little cooking. It carries strong flavours with ease and is brilliant paired with spices like chilli and, in this case, piri piri. Piri piri is dried and ground bird's eye chilli, which is commonly used in Portuguese cuisine. The key is to keep the broccoli looking as vibrant a green as possible to make the most of the fantastic nutrients that it has to offer.

serves 4

1 tablespoon soy sauce • ½ head of broccoli (approximately 400g), chopped
½ fresh lemon • pinch of piri piri to taste (less than ¼ of a teaspoon)

Method

❋ Pour the soy sauce into a wide frying pan with 60ml of water and bring to a medium heat. Tumble in the broccoli and stir well so that each piece is coated in the soy/water mixture.

❋ Increase the heat so that the liquid starts to evaporate. Grate the rind of the lemon into the frying pan on top of the broccoli.

❋ Once the liquid has gone, remove the broccoli from the pan and season to taste with the piri piri and some salt and pepper.

❋ Squeeze the fresh lemon juice on top and serve immediately.

Honey and Mustard Dressing

The beauty of keeping on top of your store cupboard supplies is that you can pull together dressings and rubs in a short amount of time. The only ingredient in this dressing that doesn't keep for long is the lemon juice. Used for salads, warm potatoes or meat, I drizzle this on anything that needs a bit of oomph or to remind me of the sun when it's missing – as it commonly is in our climate!

makes just under 50ml – enough to dress a salad for 5

2 teaspoons wholegrain mustard • 1 tablespoon extra virgin olive oil

1 tablespoon balsamic vinegar • 1 tablespoon lemon juice

1 teaspoon sugar/honey

Method

❀ Pour all the ingredients into a clean jam jar with a sealable lid and season with salt and pepper. Tighten the lid firmly and shake the bejeepers out of the jar until all the ingredients are combined.

❀ This dressing will keep for up to a week in the fridge.

Home-made Poppadoms with Spiced Onions

I've been on a quest to replace shop-bought poppadoms for a long time. I love the flavour but not the price. I also don't like that they tend to be incredibly oily. Small wonder, as they are traditionally a fried treat. I've pared this dish right back and bake mine in the oven. They are delicious with the spiced onion relish described below.

serves 4

for the poppadoms

100g gram (chickpea) flour • 25g rice flour, plus extra for dusting
1 teaspoon paprika • 1 teaspoon turmeric • pinch of salt
20g nigella (black onion) seeds • 1 tablespoon sunflower oil

for the spiced onion relish

1 small white onion, peeled and finely chopped • 2 tablespoons cider vinegar
pinch of salt • 1 tablespoon nigella seeds
1 teaspoon paprika • 1 sprig of mint, finely chopped

Method

✻ Combine all the ingredients for the spiced onion relish and cover. Leave to one side until ready to serve. Ideally prepare this the day before and allow it to ferment slightly.

✻ Mix all the poppadom ingredients together in a bowl with 30ml of water. Combine with a fork until you get a thick paste. Knead it a little and it will become a dough. Cover and chill for 20 minutes.

✻ Preheat a fan oven to 200°C.

✻ Line a baking tray with non-stick greaseproof paper.

✻ Dust a clean, smooth surface (I use my kitchen table) and a rolling pin with rice flour. Take small, pea-sized pieces of the dough and roll them as thin as you possibly can. Dust liberally to stop them from sticking. Place the rolled out dough on the baking tray and bake for 12 minutes. Serve with the spiced onion relish.

Roast Potatoes

I like to keep the skins on my roast potatoes unless it's the height of winter and the potatoes aren't in great condition. The key to great roasties is to parboil the spuds first. When making roast potatoes, our spud of choice is normally the rooster. The skin is bright red and thick when they are a long time harvested, but young roosters have a light skin. Depending on the time of the year, I leave the skins on and simply scrub the potatoes well. After all, the skin holds plenty of nutrients so it seems like a waste to throw it away.

serves 4 generously

10 medium potatoes, peeled if necessary • 4 tablespoons sunflower oil

Method

❄ Preheat a fan oven to 160°C, although as I usually make these roast potatoes to go with a roast chicken the oven is already on!

❄ Once the chicken is in the oven, I chop the potatoes into halves or quarters and place in a large pot with cold water. Bring to the boil and simmer for 10 minutes before straining the water away.

❄ Heat a large, ovenproof dish in the oven with 4 tablespoons of sunflower oil. Toss the strained and still warm, partially cooked potatoes in the hot oil carefully. Cook for 80 minutes, by which time both the chicken and roast potatoes should be cooked! Season before serving.

Roasted Tomatoes

The problem with tomatoes on the vine is that if you don't eat them within three days of buying them they go slightly squishy. But instead of throwing them out, they are now perfect for roasting. By roasting on the vine you create a more intense tomato flavour. Use a fork to mash up the cooked tomatoes making a beautiful strong flavoured sauce, which is the perfect accompaniment to steak or lamb.

serves 2

1 handful of cherry tomatoes on the vine • 2 tablespoons olive oil (regular is fine)

Method

❉ Preheat a fan oven to 180°C.

❉ Put the tomatoes and olive oil into a small roasting dish and spoon the oil over the tomatoes, so that they are well coated. Sprinkle with cracked black pepper and sea salt.

❉ Roast for 30 minutes.

❉ Remove from the oven and allow them to cool slightly.

❉ Discard the vine stems before mashing loosely with a fork and serving, or you can serve these on the stems and let everyone mash them on their plate.

Crunchy Seeds

I always keep a jar of toasted seeds in the kitchen. I either eat them by the handful, as they are a very nutritious snack and full of healthy oils and vitamins, or I sprinkle them on top of bakes and salads to add texture. The key to keeping these seeds fresh is to toast each separately and then combine the mixture you like.

ingredients

50g sunflower seeds • 50g sesame seeds • 30g poppy seeds

Method

❉ Heat a dry, shallow frying pan on a medium heat for 5 minutes. Pour the sunflower seeds in first, use a spatula to lightly toss the seeds. Once they start to brown, remove from the heat and pour into a heatproof dish to cool. This will take a while as they hold onto their heat well.

❉ Repeat for the sesame seeds and poppy seeds in turn. The poppy seeds won't brown but you will know that they are toasted as all the seeds will 'pop' and shift in the pan from the heat about 30 seconds before they are ready.

❉ When cool, combine together and store in a clean dry jar for up to a week if you can resist that long.

Tomato Relish

When it comes to spreading a relish on a cheese sandwich or stirring it into mayonnaise for a tomato dressing with a kick, I'd rather make my own inexpensively than pay for a jar that costs at least twice as much in the shop.

The perfect relish for me is a combination of sweet, sour and peppery, with a little bit of salty flavour in the background. Tomatoes are a great ingredient to make relish with, as tinned tomatoes are cheap to buy and carry flavours well.

fills a 300ml jar

1 tablespoon sunflower oil • 1 brown onion, finely chopped
½ teaspoon dried brown mustard seeds • ½ teaspoon cayenne pepper
2 tablespoons raisins • 400g tin of whole tomatoes in their own juice
1 teaspoon golden syrup • rind and juice of ½ unwaxed orange
½ teaspoon sea salt • ½ teaspoon pepper

Method

❋ Bring the sunflower oil to a medium heat in a large, wide-bottomed saucepan.

❋ Pour in the onion and mustard seeds. Stir until the mustard seeds start to pop, then add the cayenne pepper and raisins. Stir until the raisins are coated in the spice mixture.

❋ Pour in the remaining ingredients. Stir well. Bring to a simmer, cover the saucepan and leave to simmer for 1 hour. After 1 hour all the ingredients should have softened. Using a potato masher, squash everything in the saucepan. Increase the heat and reduce the liquid until it becomes a thick relish. Decant into a heated sterilised jar and seal well. Providing the jar is sterilised, the relish will keep in a cool, dark press for up to six months. Upon opening, keep the jar in the fridge and consume within the month.

Tzatziki

This is a cooling dip for fresh vegetables on a summer's day and also makes a lovely side dish when you're eating spicy food.

serves 4

½ cucumber
200ml natural yoghurt
bunch of fresh mint
vegetables to serve

Method

✿ Slice the cucumber in half lengthways and, using a teaspoon, scoop out the seeds. You won't need them for this recipe.

✿ Slice the cucumber as thinly as you possibly can. If it's an older cucumber you may like to peel off some of the skin as it can be a bit tough.

✿ Chop the mint finely.

✿ Stir the cucumber, mint and yoghurt together, before serving with chopped, crunchy vegetables such as more cucumber, pepper, carrots and celery. You may also enjoy this dip with sesame crackers (p. 81).

Sweet Treats

It's a common misconception that if you're on a budget you have to cut back on treats. My waistline is a big giveaway that we don't compromise on sweet treats around here. Baking your own treats or making them will save you money on premium cakes and biscuits. You're also able to monitor the sugar you consume and lower the overall processed foods that are in your diet. While Marie Antoinette suggested that the peasants eat 'brioche' (not cake), which is a fortified bread, there's no reason why you shouldn't brighten up the diet with some sweet treats every now and again.

Shortcake

Brittle biscuits that give a satisfying snap without too much sugar content can be hard to come by. My secret may be a surprise to many: I add a small amount of rice flour to my biscuit dough before baking. It results in a crumbly brisk texture but without the heavy sweet aftertaste.

makes about 10

50g butter at room temperature • 50g caster sugar • 1 medium egg
100g plain flour • 50g rice flour • ½ teaspoon baking powder
½ teaspoon vanilla extract (or the seeds from 1 vanilla pod)

Method

❉ Cream the butter and sugar together until they are well mixed. A hand-held electric mixer is ideal for this, but it can be done with a wooden spoon and a bit of elbow grease. Once well combined they will become light and fluffy; the volume will nearly double.

❉ Beat in the egg, then beat in the two flours, baking powder and vanilla extract until you get a stiff dough.

❉ Cover with cling film and chill in the fridge for at least 3 hours.

❉ Preheat a fan oven to 160°C.

❉ Line a baking tray with non-stick greaseproof paper.

❉ Roll out the dough into a long rectangle about 2cm thick and then cut into equal-sized pieces. Transfer each biscuit carefully onto the baking tray and then prick with a fork a couple of times.

❉ Bake in the oven for 12 minutes or until golden. Allow the biscuits to cool before serving.

Banana Butterscotch Cake

The butterscotch sauce on top of this cake gives it a really decadent feel, but if you're in a hurry, make the main cake and enjoy it on its own, without the sauce. The combination of golden syrup in the cake and the sauce on top make it sticky and gooey – all the things I love for a winter pudding.

for the cake

60g caster sugar • 125g unsalted butter, softened • 50g golden syrup
2 medium eggs • 175g plain flour • 75g wholemeal flour • 1 teaspoon baking powder
2 teaspoons ground ginger • 100g oats • 4 ripe bananas

for the butterscotch sauce

100g caster sugar • 50g butter • 25ml cream • 1 ripe banana

Method

❊ Preheat a fan oven to 170°C.

❊ Grease and flour a 1kg (2lb) loaf tin extremely well. If you do this properly, then the loaf will slide straight out.

❊ Beat together the sugar, butter and golden syrup with a hand-held electric mixer until they are well combined. The batter will become light, fluffy and nearly double in size.

❊ Add the eggs and beat well: the mixture will curdle slightly, but don't worry as this will be fixed once you add the flour.

❊ Pour in the flours, baking powder and ground ginger. Beat well again and you will get a stiff mixture.

❊ Add the oats and mix again.

❊ Peel and slice the bananas. Mix gently into the batter.

❊ Pour the batter into your prepared loaf tin. Use a spoon to make a small well down the middle of the mixture in the tin. This will allow the cake to rise and bake evenly.

❊ Bake for 50 minutes in the preheated oven. Test the cake using a skewer or cocktail stick. If it comes out clean it is ready. If the skewer is sticky, bake the cake for a further 10 minutes before testing again.

❊ Remove the cake from the oven and allow it to stand in the tin for 20 minutes before tipping out onto a cooling rack.

❊ To make the butterscotch sauce, place the sugar in a small saucepan and place on a medium heat, but do not stir it. When the sugar begins to bubble and change to a golden colour, carefully add in cubes of the butter. Stir well and then pour in the cream.

❊ Allow to simmer for 3–5 minutes until it becomes thick and unctuous. Remove from the heat.

❊ Peel the banana and slice into the sauce and flip until the slices are coated in the butterscotch. Pour over the top of the cooling banana cake and serve as an after dinner treat while the sauce is still warm, with a splash of cream or a dollop of Greek yoghurt.

Black Forest Cupcakes

I love black forest gateau, but it involves using kirsch, which I never have in the house, and I can't justify buying it for special occasions only. The boys don't really like cream and so they eat these cakes without the topping.

I make these cupcakes rich with the addition of a little rum instead of kirsch. I use fresh cherries when they're in season, but when they're not, the tinned variety works just as well.

makes 12

90g butter • 120g caster sugar • 100g golden syrup • 2 medium eggs
100g plain flour • 35g cocoa powder • 1 teaspoon baking powder
40g ground almonds • 2 tablespoons rum • 70g dark chocolate, melted and
cooled slightly • 80g fresh or tinned cherries, pitted

to decorate

200ml fresh cream
1 teaspoon rum and 1 tablespoon of icing sugar (optional)
12 cherries • chocolate chips

Method

❀ Preheat a fan oven to 170°C and line a twelve-hole cupcake tin/muffin tray with paper cases.

❀ Cream the butter, caster sugar and golden syrup together until light and fluffy.

❀ Add the eggs individually and beat well until you have a light mixture.

❀ Fold in the flour, cocoa powder, baking powder and ground almonds. Mix until well incorporated.

❀ Pour in the rum and stir. Slowly add the melted chocolate while mixing so that you don't end up with scrambled eggs. Stir in the cherries.

❀ Divide the mixture equally between the cupcake cases, taking care not to fill the cases more than three-quarters full.

❀ Bake for 25 minutes. Test with a cocktail stick. If it comes out clean, remove the cupcakes from the oven and leave to cool on a wire rack. If not, bake for a further 5 minutes before checking again.

❀ To serve, whip the cream and spoon or pipe on to the top of the cooled cupcakes. For an extra kick, add the rum and icing sugar when whipping, but if you do this make sure the kids don't get their hands on them! Sprinkle the top of the cream with chocolate chips and serve with a whole cherry on top.

Mint Chocolate 'Bark'

Do you ever get those sticks of rock from friends and family who have been on holidays? Or those candy canes that linger at the back of the Christmas tree and you wonder how the kids missed them? Well now you have the perfect way to get rid of them.

I love chocolate and mint together. I can't really call this a recipe because it's so simple, but the combination of the sweets and the dark chocolate make for a festive treat or gift.

ingredients

200g good quality dark chocolate
1 stick of rock/2 candy canes/200g mint boiled sweets

Method

❉ Cover a baking tray with cling film and place in the fridge.

❉ Melt the chocolate in a heatproof bowl over a pot of hot water.

❉ Unwrap the rock/canes/sweets, then put in a sandwich bag and bash the bejeepers out of the contents using a rolling pin until you have shards of mintyness.

❉ Remove the tin from the fridge and carefully pour the melted chocolate onto it. Tumble the shards of sweets on top, distributing them as evenly as possible. Once the chocolate has reached room temperature return the tray to the fridge for 30 minutes.

❉ Break the chocolate 'bark' into chunks and eat, wrap up prettily to give as a gift, or return to the fridge for a treat for another day.

Simple Cookies

I could make these cookies in my sleep. The kids love them and love me even more because I bring them to school events and fairs to share!

The trick with cookies is to make loads, chill the dough, then roll the balls and freeze them in bags. That way you can remove them from the freezer and cook the exact amount you want. Add a handful of chocolate chips or raisins to the mixture if you like.

makes 20

125g butter, softened • 125g caster sugar • 1 medium egg
1 teaspoon vanilla extract • 250g plain flour • ½ teaspoon baking powder

Method

✿ Cream together the butter and sugar until light and fluffy with a beating paddle on a stand mixer or with a steady arm and a wooden spoon.

✿ Beat in the egg until the batter returns to its fluffy state, add the vanilla extract and beat a little more. Sieve in the flour and baking powder, then beat again. This requires elbow grease, as there is so much flour it gets very stiff. Once fully mixed, spoon into a sandwich bag and chill for 3 hours.

✿ Once chilled, roll balls of dough the size of a ping-pong ball in your hands.

✿ To freeze: sit on baking paper on a baking tray or plate with a little space between each dough ball. Freeze for 3 hours (I do this overnight), then, once solid, pour into a sandwich bag. The dough will keep for up to 3 months in the bottom of the freezer away from the element.

✿ To cook: preheat a fan oven to 190°C and line a baking tray with non-stick baking parchment. Space the dough balls evenly on the baking tray – approximately five per tray is best as otherwise they spread into one another and you'll end up with one giant cookie! Bake for 8 minutes if fresh or 12 minutes from frozen until golden brown. I prefer to cook from frozen as you get a smoother finish on the biscuit.

✿ Remove them from the oven and allow to cool for 10 minutes before lifting with a spatula and cooling further on a rack. Serve with a glass of cold milk.

Eton Mess Cake

I keep frozen berries in the bottom of my freezer all year around as they are brilliant for baking. Eton mess is an old-fashioned dessert traditionally made with cream, strawberries and meringue pieces, but this cake version can be made with a variety of berries. There is a recipe for pavlova on page 237, if you want to make the meringue from scratch. Alternatively you will find meringue nests on special in most big supermarkets just after Christmas. Stock up – they have a long shelf-life and are handy for a cake like this.

serves at least 8

125g butter, softened • 150g caster sugar • 3 medium eggs
250g plain flour • 1 teaspoon baking powder
100g strawberries (fresh or frozen is fine)
100g meringue, crumbled

for the topping

100g fresh strawberries, chopped • 100g meringue, crumbled
100ml fresh cream, whipped

Method

❋ Preheat a fan oven to 170°C. Grease and flour a 22cm bundt tin.

❋ Cream the butter and sugar together with a hand-held electric mixer until light and fluffy.

❋ Beat in the eggs one by one until the mixture is fluffy again. If it becomes a little scrambled in appearance, add a spoonful of the flour.

❋ Beat in the flour and baking powder. Finally stir in the strawberries and meringue pieces.

❋ Pour into the prepared tin and bake for 40 minutes. Test with a skewer – if it comes out clean, then it is baked. Otherwise bake for a further 5 minutes and repeat.

❋ Allow the cake to cool in the tin for 20 minutes before putting a cooling rack over the top and gently tipping it out of the tin. Use a non-stick spatula to help.

❋ Transfer to a serving plate and fill the centre of the cake with the meringue pieces, strawberries and whipped cream.

Grapefruit Mini Loaf with Sesame Brittle

You will find the sesame brittle recipe on page 230. You need to make it, if only to try this very special recipe when you can get pink grapefruit in the shops!

makes 8 individual loaves

220g butter • 220g caster sugar • 4 medium eggs • 200g plain flour
2 teaspoons baking powder
segments of 1 pink grapefruit with the pith removed (prepare this over a bowl so
that you can catch any juice for use in the icing)

for the icing

150g icing sugar • 25ml grapefruit juice

Method

- Use mini-loaf tins if you have them. Otherwise you can make this as a layered cake by baking it in two 18cm sandwich tins. Line the tins you're going to use with non-stick greaseproof paper and preheat a fan oven to 170°C.

- Cream the butter and sugar together with a hand-held electric mixer, add the eggs one by one, beating after each addition. Make sure you mix them in completely. Add a little of the flour if you think it's becoming curdled.

- Sieve in the flour and baking powder. Beat again, then stir in the grapefruit segments.

- Divide the mixture between the lined baking tins. Bake in the oven for 25 minutes if making the mini loaves or 35 minutes for the sandwich tins. Test with a skewer – if it comes out clean remove the cakes from the oven and allow to cool. If not, return to the oven and bake for a further 7 minutes before testing again.

- Allow the cakes to cool in the tins for a few minutes before tipping out onto a rack to cool completely.

- Ice the cakes by dissolving the icing sugar in the grapefruit juice with a little squished segment. Drizzle over the loaves and sprinkle the top with some broken sesame brittle. If making a sandwich cake, put half the icing and brittle between the layers and half on top.

Macaroons

Macaroons, not to be confused with their glamorous French cousins 'macarons', are simple coconutty pleasures that disappeared in a blink of an eye when I brought them to a school party. They are so simple to make, require no use of electric mixers and are easy for children of any age to assemble with a little supervision.

makes about 8 small ones

100g caster sugar • 1 medium egg white • 150g dried coconut
more caster sugar for dredging

Method

❊ Preheat a fan oven to 170°C. Line a baking tray with a sheet of non-stick greaseproof paper.

❊ Combine the sugar, egg white and coconut with a fork in a large bowl, until you get a sticky paste.

❊ Wet your hands and shape the mixture into little balls. Put the balls on the baking tray and shake a little more caster sugar over the top.

❊ Bake in the oven for 20 minutes, or until golden. Allow to cool before lifting them off the paper, otherwise they will stick.

Mince Tart

Christmas comes around and everybody looks forward to a mince pie. I prefer to make these open mince tarts, which look incredibly pretty. They are not hard to make at all and if you make your own home-made sweet mince they can be very frugal.

makes 4 open mince tarts which serve 2 people each

270g roll of ready-made chilled puff pastry • 200g mincemeat • 1 medium egg
small amount of sugar for sprinkling • whipped cream to serve

Method

❀ Preheat a fan oven to 170°C. Line a baking tray with non-stick baking parchment.

❀ Using a 15cm side plate, trace out circles on the pastry. I normally get four from a roll. Use a sharp knife to score a series of crescents radiating from a central point to the edge of the pastry. This allows the pastry to cook evenly and prevents the tarts going soggy.

❀ Flip the pastry over onto the baking tray and fill the middle of the pastry circle with one quarter of the sweet mincemeat. Using your fingers pull the edges of the pastry up and squeeze to create a ruffled edge. Beat the egg and brush a little on the exposed pastry, then sprinkle the wet edges with sugar.

❀ Bake for 25 minutes until golden brown and crispy.

❀ Serve warm or cold with fresh whipped cream.

Porter Cake

I always remember eating porter cake with lashings of Irish butter. It's a real treat and I like to make mine with wholemeal flour, which adds a nutty flavour to the cake.

makes 1 cake

200ml porter, e.g. Guinness or Murphy's

100g dried fruit – I like to use cranberries, raisins, sultanas and currants

100g butter, softened • 75g brown sugar • 2 medium eggs • 150g plain flour

150g wholemeal flour • 1 teaspoon baking powder

Method

❉ Preheat a fan oven to 170°C. Grease a 2lb (1kg) loaf tin and dust with flour.

❉ Pour the porter over the dried fruit, cover and leave to stand overnight for the best results.

❉ Cream the butter and sugar together – you're not trying to add air here so just make sure they are well mixed. Beat in the eggs one by one. Beat in the two flours and the baking powder. Strain off any remaining liquid from soaking the fruit and beat that into the cake mixture. Finally stir in the strained fruit.

❉ Pour the cake batter into your prepared cake tin. Bake in the oven for 45 minutes. Check the cake is cooked using a skewer and if it doesn't come out clean, bake for a further 5 minutes and repeat.

❉ Wait until the cake is cool before tipping out and serving in slices with a slather of Irish butter.

Sesame Brittle

How can two simple ingredients combine to create such a tasty treat?

You'll see little packages of brittle in the supermarket. They're packed full of sugars and in fairness so is my recipe. However, I haven't messed around with things like high fructose corn syrup, which is incredibly bad for you. Remember the less that goes into your treats the better! You can eat a small amount of sesame brittle for a combination of energy and protein at once. Not too much though!

makes enough brittle for 10 lunchboxes (if you can stop them from eating it all at once?)

100g caster sugar • 150g sesame seeds

Method

❋ Take a large, heavy-bottomed saucepan and pour the caster sugar and a little dribble of water in the bottom. Start with a low heat and gradually increase the heat until you have a bubbling liquid sugar. Don't be tempted to stir or touch. Sugar is like molten lava and it will crystallise if you touch it too much.

❋ While it is heating, you need to prepare a smooth surface. Greased tinfoil shiny side up works well. I happen to have a piece of marble in the kitchen that comes in very handy.

❋ When the sugar is bubbling, turn the heat down and wait for it to turn a golden colour. As soon as you see a golden colour, stir in the sesame seeds. They will begin to pop and cook. Stir for exactly 2 minutes more, then carefully pour the mixture onto your smooth surface.

❋ This brittle is hot so handle very carefully. As soon as you pour it out it will begin to cool. As soon as the liquid beomes solid (this will take about 4 minutes) use a spatula to turn it over so that the other side rests on the smooth surface to make it shiny, then leave to cool completely before breaking into bite-sized pieces.

Apple Strudel

Apple tart gets rolled out at every opportunity in our house. It's my grandad's favourite and in fact on our wedding day, my hubby and he enjoyed a slice to themselves rather than having the dessert on offer!

I don't always have the time to roll out pastry, blind bake and cut it to fit, so a strudel is a handier and quicker way to make up a tart without much mess or hassle.

serves 8

270g roll of ready-made chilled puff pastry • 4 Granny Smith apples
1 handful of dried fruit • 2 tablespoons golden caster sugar

Method

❀ Preheat a fan oven to 170°C. Line a baking tray with non-stick greaseproof paper.

❀ Unroll the puff pastry over the baking tray, leaving a 5cm space on the right-hand side of the tray. It will overhang the other side of the tray for the moment but don't worry.

❀ Peel, core and slice the apples in chunks directly onto the pastry on the right hand side only, leaving about 2½cm to the edge of the pastry. This will allow for turning later. Sprinkle the dried fruit and caster sugar on top.

❀ Fold the empty portion of the pastry over the filling. Using your finger rub a tiny bit of water around the edges and then pinch and roll the edges to seal the parcel. Score the top with a sharp knife.

❀ Bake for 35 minutes or until golden brown. Dust with icing sugar to serve if you like.

Marmalade Cake

Marmalade adds a fabulous tart hit to this cake. It's handy when you don't have a lot of ingredients in the house as you can lash it together pretty quickly.

makes 8 generous pieces

125g butter, softened • 150g caster sugar • 3 medium eggs
200g plain flour • 1 teaspoon baking powder
100g marmalade, plus a tablespoon for drizzling

Method

❀ Preheat a fan oven to 170°C. Grease and dust a 22cm bundt tin with flour.

❀ Cream the butter and sugar together with a hand-held electric mixer until light and fluffy, then add the eggs one by one. Beat in the flour and baking powder. Stir in the marmalade. Spoon the cake mixture into the bundt tin.

❀ Bake for 35 minutes. Check with a skewer to see if it comes away clean. If not, bake for a further 5 minutes and test again.

❀ Remove from the oven and allow it to cool slightly before turning out gently.

❀ To serve, mix a little more marmalade with a little hot water to make it runny and drizzle it over the top.

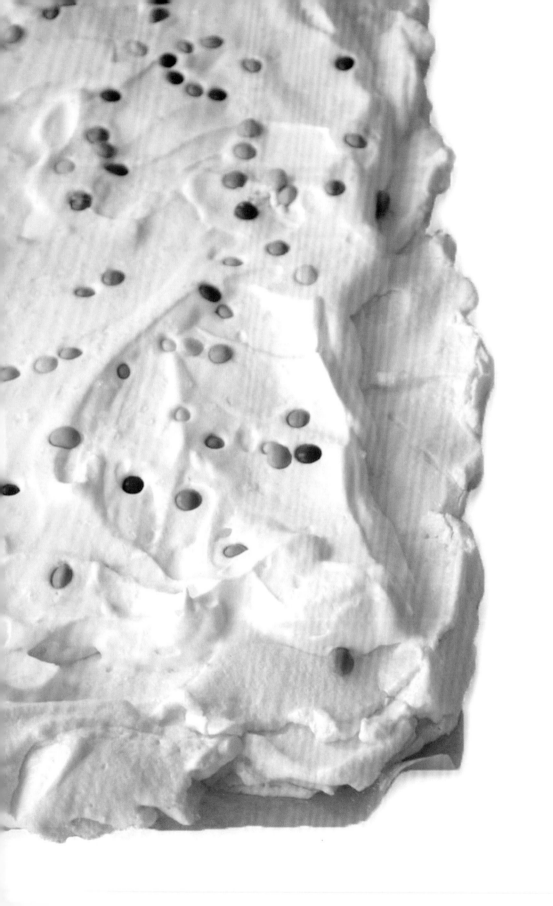

Pavlova

No matter what the family party, I will be asked to bring a pavlova. You'll find recipes here and there using various different ingredients, but you won't find anything complicated here. Simple is always better when it comes to making meringues. The key to the taste and flavour is the drying process. I always recommend that you make a pavlova the night before you intend to eat it and leave it to dry out in the oven overnight.

The only difficulty with making a pavlova by hand is that you will get tired pretty quickly. I always recommend some form of electric whisk to make life easier on yourself.

serves 6

3 egg whites • 90g caster sugar
200ml whipping cream • fruit or chocolate to decorate

Method

❊ Preheat a fan oven to 130°C. Line a baking tray with non-stick greaseproof paper. Use a plate and a pencil to mark out a large circle on the sheet.

❊ In a clean bowl whisk the egg whites until you get stiff, tall peaks. Tablespoon by tablespoon, add the caster sugar, whisking all the time. Continue whisking until you get glossy stiff peaks.

❊ Take a metal spoon and spread the mixture onto the baking tray, making sure to stay within the circle you've marked. Don't worry too much about smoothing it down. The crinkly peaks and troughs will add crunchiness when baking.

❊ Bake for 2 hours, then reduce the temperature to 100°C. Bake for a further hour. Don't open the oven at any time.

❊ Turn the oven off and leave overnight.

❊ Decorate with whipped cream and chocolate or fruit (or both!), then serve.

Cheat's Trifle

At least one drawer of my freezer is always full of frozen berries. I either pick up fresh berries when they're on special, pick the likes of blackberries in the autumn or buy a bag of frozen berries as they can be incredibly cheap. This is a cheat's quick trifle that the kids love to eat with big spoons.

serves 6

200g frozen berries (fresh is fine too) • 50ml fresh squeezed orange juice
1 teaspoon ground ginger • 100g nibbed almonds • 50g butter, melted
1 medium egg • 150g ground almonds • 1 drop almond flavouring
¼ teaspoon baking powder • 300ml vanilla yoghurt

Method

✳ Place the berries, orange juice and ground ginger in a medium saucepan, bring to a simmer for 5 minutes and then set to one side.

✳ Toast the nibbed almonds under the grill or in a dry frying pan until golden brown but not black.

✳ Take a large microwave-proof dish and mix the butter, egg, ground almonds, almond flavouring and baking powder with a fork until you get a paste. Microwave for 1 minute on high. Leave to stand for 3 minutes. Microwave for another minute, stand for 3 minutes and repeat one more time.

✳ To assemble, take a big bowl or a number of small glasses. Put spoonfuls of the stewed fruit on the bottom, then top with the almond 'sponge'. It doesn't matter if it's a bit tough as it's going to soak into the fruit juices. Top with spoonfuls of fresh vanilla yoghurt and then the toasted nibbed almonds.

Gooseberry Fool

While gooseberry fool is a very seasonal treat for the middle of the summer when gooseberries are ripe, you can enjoy fool all year round – just change the type of fruit you use, or use frozen gooseberries.

serves 5

200g fresh gooseberries • 3 tablespoons sugar • 200ml milk
1 teaspoon vanilla extract • 2 egg yolks • 1 tablespoon cornflour
150ml fresh cream

Method

❊ Put the gooseberries and 2 tablespoons of the sugar in a small saucepan and heat on low. Leave to simmer gently until all the fruit has popped. Once it has popped, mash with a potato masher, then strain away the larger pieces through a sieve.

❊ Heat the milk in a large saucepan along with the vanilla extract. Put the egg yolks, cornflour and the remaining tablespoon of sugar in a mug and stir with a fork. When the milk is warm, pour this mixture into the milk and whisk well. Continue to lightly whisk the milk as it comes to the boil. Keep on whisking until it becomes thick and fluffy. Remove from the heat and allow to cool.

❊ Once all the ingredients are cold, whip the cream to loose peaks. Pour half the whipped cream into the custard mixture and stir with a spoon. Pour in the gooseberry sauce. Stir again and then fold in the rest of the cream.

❊ Serve immediately in individual glasses/cups.

Jam Tarts

There isn't much of a science to making jam tarts, but knowing how to make good short-crust pastry is very handy in the kitchen.

makes 4 large jam tarts

75g cold butter • 150g plain flour • Ice-cold water
Flour for dusting • Jam of your choice

Method

* Dice the butter and mix it together with the flour using a knife, or a fork. If you have a food processor then use it and make a larger batch. This pastry freezes very well.

* The flour should begin to come together with the butter a little, but remain in breadcrumb-sized pieces. Add a tablespoon of the ice-cold water and mix again. Continue adding water gradually until the dough begins to form a big lump. Pull the dough together with your hands into a ball. Cover with cling film and chill in the fridge for at least an hour.

* Preheat a fan oven to 180°C. Grease four 18cm baking tins well and dust them with flour. If you only have two tins you can make two batches.

* Dust a clean, smooth surface with flour and roll out the dough. Cut to the size you need and pop into the prepared baking tin. Cover the baking tin with greaseproof paper and fill with dry rice.

* Bake in the oven for 25 minutes. Remove and carefully lift the paper with the rice out of the pastry shell. Fill the shell with the jam of your choice up to ¾ of the height of the shell. Bake again in the oven for a further 15 minutes.

* Allow the tart to cool before serving.

Double Espresso Cake

We all love coffee cake. I've reduced the amount of sugar that I use in the cake, and use a mixture of plain and coarse wheat flour in this recipe. The coffee flavour sings through.

serves 8

125g butter, softened • 100g caster sugar • 2 medium eggs • 100g plain flour
100g coarse wholemeal flour • 1 teaspoon baking powder • 1 shot of espresso

for the frosting

125g unsalted butter • 175g icing sugar • 1 shot of espresso
walnuts or chocolate to decorate

Method

* Preheat a fan oven to 170°C. Line two 18cm sandwich tins with non-stick greaseproof paper.

* Beat the butter and sugar together with a hand-held electric mixer until light and fluffy.

* Add in the eggs one at a time, beating each time until they are well combined.

* Pour in the flours and baking powder. Beat well again until you get a stiff batter.

* Add the espresso and beat again – the batter will become looser.

* Divide the mixture between the two tins and bake in the oven for 35 minutes. Remove from the tin and allow the cakes to cool on a rack before removing any lining paper that may have stuck to them.

* For the frosting, beat the butter and icing sugar together until pale and fluffy. Pour in the espresso and beat again, it will become quite loose.

* Sandwich the two cakes together with some of the icing and spread lashings of it on top. Decorate with chocolate or walnuts.

Peanut-Butter Refrigerator Cake

Refrigerator cake is so easy to make, the only reason why we don't have more of it is because I never have enough space in my fridge. The most classic recipes use lots of sugar and chocolate, and while I love them, this is an alternative using no extra sugar and peanut butter instead. The beauty of refrigerator cake is that there is no baking at all involved in making it. In fact, technically it's not really a cake at all. All you need to do is crumble the dry ingredients into some melted, wet ingredients, then mix together and leave to set before slicing or serving.

serves 5

15 digestive biscuits
4 tablespoons peanut butter
1 handful of roasted peanuts

Method

❈ Line a baking tray with cling film and make sure you have space for it in your fridge.

❈ Put the biscuits in a large sandwich bag and bash them until you have a fine meal. The kids love doing this in my house.

❈ Take a large saucepan and heat the peanut butter until it becomes runny. Pour in the ground biscuits and coat in the peanut butter. Press into the lined tin, then sprinkle the roasted peanuts on top. Press down with the back of a spoon to get them to stick to the mixture.

❈ Cover the top with cling film. Chill the cake for at least 2 hours before slicing and serving.

Mint Chocolate Brownie Cake

Classic birthday cakes in our house are made of sponge and icing, but this is a decadent, squidgy mess. Trust me, this is a good thing when it comes to cakes! If you don't like the combination of chocolate and mint, then use another flavour – vanilla works extremely well, but almond or orange would also work.

The trick to assembling the cake is to make sure each brownie layer is frozen before putting them together with the icing, otherwise you'll end up with a large (but delicious) pile of crumbs. Use skewers to hold the cake in one place before cutting.

serves 20

200g dark chocolate • 150g butter • 200g caster sugar • 4 eggs • 100g plain flour
75g cocoa powder • 1 teaspoon baking powder

for the frosting

500g icing sugar • 225g unsalted butter at room temperature
2 teaspoons peppermint extract • melted chocolate to decorate

Method

❉ Preheat a fan oven to 170°C. Line four 18cm sandwich tins with non-stick greaseproof paper. If you only have two tins you can make the cake in two batches.

❉ Melt the chocolate and butter together in a large bowl over a pot of hot water.

❉ Whisk the sugar and eggs together with an electric whisk, until they are light, creamy and have nearly trebled in size. Slowly pour the melted chocolate and butter into the whisked eggs while whisking on high. It will become steamy!

❉ Fold in the flour, cocoa powder and baking powder and stir until combined. Divide the mixture between the sandwich tins and bake in the oven for 35 minutes. Remove from the tin and allow to cool on a wire rack, then wrap individually with greaseproof paper or cling film and freeze for at least 1 hour.

❉ To make the frosting, beat the icing sugar, unsalted butter and peppermint extract until it has doubled in size.

❉ Use the frosting to sandwich the frozen cake pieces together and pour melted chocolate over the top. Allow to come to room temperature before serving.

No-Cook Chocolate Pudding

While you aren't 'cooking' this chocolate pudding, the hot melted chocolate technically cooks the eggs, so it is safer to eat. It is also extremely addictive.

serves 6

100g dark chocolate • 75g butter • 2 medium eggs • 100g caster sugar

Method

❄ Melt the chocolate and butter together in a large heatproof glass bowl suspended over a pot of hot water.

❄ Mix the eggs and sugar together in a large mixing bowl with a hand-held electric whisk, until light and frothy. They will double in size.

❄ Once the chocolate and butter have melted, stir to make sure they are mixed together well. Turn the whisk on high and slowly, bit by bit, drip the chocolate mixture into the whipped egg. Steam will rise off as the chocolate cooks the egg. Continue to whisk on as high a setting as you can until all the chocolate has been mixed in, then whisk for another 3 minutes before pouring into six individual pots and chilling.

❄ Now you can eat the pudding warm, but I'd recommend chilling for about 2 hours before eating, if you can wait that long!

Wholesome Meal Plan

	Breakfast	Lunch	Dinner	Snacks/Treats
Monday	Guggy Egg with Toast	Hummus	Roast Chicken (make double vegetable quantities for Tuesday's Chicken Stuffing Bake)	Bananas Apples Pears Oranges Sultanas Apricots Prunes Raisins Simple Cookies Macaroons
Tuesday	Blueberry Muffins	Family Salad Jar	Chicken Stuffing Bake	
Wednesday	Brown Bread & Marmalade	Home-made Baked Beans	Pea Risotto	
Thursday	Pop Tarts	Broccoli Soup	Lamb Burger with Cucumber Pickle	
Friday	Porridge	Tuna Melt	Beetroot and Ricotta Pizza	
Saturday	Pancake Pops	Bread Pesto Quesadillas	Mildly Spiced Beef Stir-Fry	
Sunday	Baked French Toast Chips	Raspberry Ricotta Scones	Three Bean Chilli	

	Breakfast	Lunch	Dinner	Snacks/Treats
Monday	Breakfast Bars	Mixed Salad	Fish Scale Pie	Sesame Brittle Grapefruit Mini-Loaf Chocolate Mint Brownie Cake Bananas Apples Pears Dried Fruit
Tuesday	Berry Smoothie	Minestrone	Sausage Casserole	
Wednesday	Brown Bread & Marmalade	Sesame Crackers	Paprika Beef with Bacon	
Thursday	Porridge	Tabbouleh	Roasted Vegetable Lasagne	
Friday	Breakfast Bars	'Mac' and Cheese	Warm Salmon Salad	
Saturday	Banana Melba Toast	Falafel	Quick Chicken Satay	
Sunday	Fruit Samosa	Chard Potatoes	Chicken Soup	

Index